Jeet Kune Do Principles
All Martial Artists Can Use

By Tim Tackett

DISCLAIMER: Please note that the author and publisher of this book are NOT RESPONSIBLE in any manner whatsoever for any injury that may result from practicing the techniques and/or following the instructions given within. Since the physical activities described herein may be too strenuous in nature for some readers to engage in safely, it is essential that a physician be consulted prior to training.

First published in 2022 by AWP LLC/Empire Books

Copyright © 2022 AWP LLC/Empire Books

All rights reserved. No part of this publication may be reproduced or utilized in any form or by any means, electronic or mechanical, including photo- copying, recording, or by any information storage and retrieval system, without prior written permission from AWP LLC/Empire Books.

EMPIRE BOOKS
P.O. Box 491788, Los Angeles, CA 90049

First Edition -- Library of Congress Catalog Number: ISBN-13: 978-1-949753-42-4

22 21 20 19 18 17 16 15 14 13 12

Library of Congress Cataloging-in-Publication Data:

Jeet Kune Do Principles / by Tim Tackett. -- 1st ed. p. cm. Includes index.
ISBN 978-1-949753-42-4 (pbk. : alk. paper) 1. Jeet kune do. 5. Martial arts--technique. 3. Large type books. I. Title. GV1332.3.F715 2014 769.815'3--dc24

Photo courtesy of Warner Brothers

"Liberating truth is a reality only in so far as it is experienced and lived by the individual himself; it is a truth that transcends styles or disciplines."

– BRUCE LEE

DEDICATION

To my wonderful wife of 61 years,
Geraldine Gros Tackett.

Thanks to those who
posed for the photos in the book:

Dennis Blue, Jeremy Lynch, Paul Kim,
Melvin Wells, Jr., and our grandchildren
Jacob, Caleb and Aleah Tackett.

ABOUT THE AUTHOR

WHILE IN THE U.S. AIR FORCE, Sifu Tackett was stationed in Taiwan for almost three years. While he was there, he studied kuo shu [kung-fu]. His wife was working as a teacher in the Taipei American school during the day and he was working in the evening at the Shu Lin Kuo Air Force Station. Since he had his days free, he started to look for something to occupy his time. One of his friends recommended that he take up martial arts. He ended up learning six hours a day for six days a week. While in Taiwan, he studied two types of Hsing-i, Tai chi, northern and southern Shaolin, White Crane, and Monkey Boxing. After his discharge from the Air Force, he continued work on his college degree. Since he had a wife and two children to support, he opened up a full-time Kung fu school in Redlands, California while starting as a junior at the University of California, Riverside campus in 1966.

In 1967 he saw Bruce Lee demonstrate JKD at Ed Parker's tournament in Long Beach, California, and wanted to start studying with him right on the spot. But he soon realized that he would not have enough time until after he finished college. In 1968, he started a Master of Fine Arts program at UCR and no longer had time to teach martial arts full-time. So, he closed down his school and rented a hall in Redlands two nights a week where he taught what he called "Chinese karate," as hardly anyone had heard of "Kung fu," let alone "Kuo shu."

In 1970 he received my M.F.A. and started teaching drama in high school. Soon after his first student, Bob Chapman, and him, on the recommendation of Dan Lee, sought out Dan Inosanto, who had opened up a backyard Jeet Kune Do school after Bruce Lee had closed his L.A. Chinatown school shortly before moving to Hong Kong to star in movies. Both men felt privileged to be accepted in Inosanto's backyard class. The class consisted of about ten students and Sifu Tackett got to meet for the first time such JKD luminaries as Bob Bremer, Dan Lee, Richard Bustillo, Jerry Poteet, and Pete Jacobs. Later Chris Kent, Ted Lucay Lucay, and Jeff Imada joined the private group of students.

In 1973, Dan Inosanto honored Tackett with the rank of "senior first" and he was given permission to have a small Jeet Kune Do group. In Dan's backyard school, it was always stressed that JKD was something special. There were certain techniques that Bruce Lee did not want given out, outside of what we all felt was a small and special group. Dan told us that Bruce said, "If knowledge is power, then why pass it out indiscriminately."

Like many Jeet Kune Do students, Tackett has received supplemental training in western boxing, Thai boxing, wrestling, and Wing Chun. He has been described by Dan Inosanto as "one of the most knowledgeable JKD instructors in the world."

Sifu Tackett was teaching the principles of JKD and using them as tools to examine the martial arts he had learned up until that time. He found that much of what he had been teaching was not very efficient. Since he didn't want to teach JKD openly, he closed the school and moved the senior group to his garage where it has been ever since.

Table of Contents

Introduction	1
The 27 Arts of Jeet Kune Do	5
Intercepting	23
Close Range Defense	35
Mobility and Stillness	47
Principles of Attack	57
The Time Commitment Theory	75
Feinting and Faking	79
Rhythm and Broken Rhythm	91
Economy of Motion	93
The 3 Stages of Combat	96

Principles of Defense	**99**
Training Methods	**105**
Sparring	**129**
Attributes	**145**
The Hammer Principle	**160**
Bruce Lee's Dragon Story	**164**
Conclusion	**167**
One-on-One with Tim Tackett	**171**

INTRODUCTION

The title of this book is *Jeet Kune Do Principles All Martial Artists can use.* In fact, most of these principles are used everyday by all martial artists, and most like speed, are not unique to JKD. The purpose of this book is to explain some of these principles and share some ideas on how to train for them. Some are principles like the use of distance in combat, while others are sayings on combat by the founder of JKD Bruce Lee to illustrate a principle.

> *"When you understand the root,
> you understand all of its blossoming."*
> – BRUCE LEE

To understand the root, you need to understand the principles. The principles of Jeet Kune are universal, but unfortunately the principles are no longer stressed as much anymore, because there is too much focus on technique alone, and seeing how many techniques you can add to your toolbox. Our Wednesday Night Group tries to have a specialized toolbox with just a few tools. At the same time, we are still searching and experimenting to see if we can find a better way to do something. We call ourselves the Wednesday Night Group, because it was on a Wednesday night when we started teaching JKD in my garage around 1975 to a small group of students. Our group still meets every Wednesday night in my garage. We now have branches all around the USA, as well as Europe and South America. I mainly write these books as a source of knowledge for our students.

Many books have been written about Jeet Kune Do. I have written a few myself, but I haven't written one that focused mainly on the Jeet Kune Do principles that makes the art really work in combat. Maybe instead of just working on, say, kicking techniques, why not try taking a principle like directness or efficiency and see how each of your kicks that work with that principle?

The purpose of this book is to discuss some of the principles that our group focuses on, and to give you some examples to illustrate those principles in action. The hope of this book is that you do the same with the main techniques you either are studying or teaching.

During his lifetime, Lee was worried that somebody somewhere would take his words and turn them into a religion, or a style that would bind future martial artists in to a straightjacket of second-hand wisdom. "It is like a finger pointing at the moon. Please do not take the finger for the moon or fix your gaze so intently on the finger that you miss all the beautiful sights of heaven. After all the usefulness of the finger is pointing away from it to all the heavenly glory" Bruce Lee

After all, when you get right down it, a better style can be considered no more than a better cage, if you are bound by it.

The 80/20 Rule

Also known as the *Prado Principle,* the 80/20 rule states that quite often 80% of your results will come from 20% of your efforts. Therefore, to achieve maximum results, you should spend 80% of your time on the 20% that matters. For our group, we try to use it to focus on the core techniques and principles of JKD in our training. The trick is figuring out exactly which techniques make up the vital 20% and that will also deliver 80% of the results. When you understand the "what, when and why" of each technique, you are on your way to knowledge that you can understand and utilize. When you are working on a particular technique you need to understand just what you are trying to accomplish. Ask yourself just what is the purpose of what I am learning, and if there is better and more efficient way to achieve the same ends? It is a constant process of refining what works and getting rid of what doesn't work. What we are looking for is what Bob Bremer called "useable knowledge" After all what good is knowledge that you are unable to use.

Bruce Lee rebelled against what he called the classical mess with its "unreal footwork and mechanical body movement". He wanted the training to be alive and not dead. He compared rhythmic form training to the broken rhythm in Western shadow boxing which he much preferred to forms. He said he wanted his martial art to be non-classical, direct, and simple. We will cover these principles and more in this book. Some I got from my Jeet Kune Do teachers, who got them directly Bruce Lee, or from things that Bruce Lee wrote himself. We will start with structure.

"I did not create a style because a style is a crystallization, and what you need is a process of continuous growth."

– BRUCE LEE

Understanding Structure

All martial arts have a specific structure. It is the structure that makes their art work. To understand any marital art, you need to understand its structure. You can think of structure as a base of operations from which the attacks and defenses of each martial art spring from. Structure is the base from which art grows. Structure is the root from which the branches of the art spring.

We look at different arts for two basic reasons. One is to see if we have the tools to defend against them. To do this we need to look at the art's structure and their delivery system. We then need to understand if we have the basic tools to deal with them. The second reason is we then need to know enough of how each art attacks from their structure to be able to practice how to defend against it. You need to be able to have your students try to enter and attack the way that other arts attack in a realistic manner and see if you can stop it.

THE 27 ARTS OF JEET KUNE DO

Not too long after Bruce Lee passed away my teacher Dan Inosanto let me go though some of the notes on JKD that Bruce Lee have given him. One of the things I came across was a paper that listed 27 different martial arts that ranged from hsing-i to hung gar and white eyebrow kung fu. When I asked Sifu Dan what this list was all about, he told me that they were just a list of some of the arts that Bruce Lee investigated to see how they entered, so he could find out if that he had the tools to stop them. It was not to see what techniques he could add to his art. Jeet Kune do is definitely not a mixture of these 27 arts. It is mainly a mixture of Wing Chun, Western Boxing, and Western fencing. This is explained in my last book, *Essential Jeet Kune Do*.

The Structure of the On-Guard Stance

The on-guard stance is the basic platform for both the JKD attack and defense.

The feet should be at least shoulder distance or a bit longer. The important thing is that you can move quickly and easily in all directions *(see photo next page)*.

The rear heal should be raised.

    1. It allows you to thrust forward quickly for a hand attack or slide up for a kicking attack.

2. You can drop your weight back to avoid a punch

3. By twisting your rear heel, you can twist your head to slip punches, and add some mobility while keeping the same distance. It will add a measure of evasiveness to your stance.

4. Your rear foot is the piston for your whole fighting machine.

5. Your weight should be balanced at about a 50-50 weight distribution, but not be static. You need to be able to switch your weight as the situation demands it. I usually have about 60% of my weight on my rear leg when stationary and waiting for any opponent to enter, so I can intercept him with a stop hit with more explosiveness when I transfer my weight to the front foot.

1. Your front hand should be aimed directly at your opponent's nose, as if your front hand has a sword in it.

2. You rear fist should be at or near you chin with the elbow down to protect your side.

3. Your rear foot is a 45-degree angle.

4. Your front foot is not straight, or at a 45-degree angle. If it is straight, your groin is too open. If it is at a 45-degree angle, you cannot extend your straight lead as far as you should for maximum power. Try to have your front foot at around a 25-degree angle.

5. Your upper body should not be square, as you will leave too much open to attack.

6. At the same time, you should not have your shoulder turned too much to the front, or you will not be able to transfer your weight to your front leg to get stopping power when you intercept with a straight lead punch.

7. Try to have your shoulders at about a 45 degree angle

Some Basic Principles

Distance: Know the Fighting Measure:

Any attack starts from a close enough distance will be able to reach you, no matter how fast you can react. Any good Western fencer understands this concept. The idea that you can be within arms reach of an experienced knife fighter and survive unharmed is a foolish and dangerous idea.

Examples:

The Fighting Measure:

This looks like a safe distance, with your hand out at full extension, it isn't really because your opponent can gain distance by twisting his rear foot, as this will transfer some his weight to his front leg. This will enable him to hit you with a finger jab without having to step forward.

The Finger Jab:

The Sequence with a Close up of the Foot Twist:
(See photo below and next page.)

You can also gain distance with a finger jab by quickly stepping up with your rear leg. Then quickly retuning back to the fighting measure. *(See photos on next page.)*

One of most important principles in JKD is learning the importance of the fighting measure. The fighting measure is that distance between you and any possible opponent where you are both just out of reach of each other's tools. This means that for an attacker to make physical contact with you, he will have to take a step forward to strike you with either a hand or foot attack.

NOTE: The two preceding sequences are exceptions to the principle that says that at the fighting measure your opponent must step forward to be able to hit you.

But except for those 2 examples, it is maintaining the fighting measure that gives you the time to react. When your opponent has stepped forward and moves within striking range, you must consider it an attack, even if he has not tried to strike. Once he has moved inside your fighting measure, he has crossed into what is called the *critical distance line.* Once your opponent has moved past this line, he will be able to strike you before you have the time to react. You then need to be able to take care of this threat as quickly and as efficiently as possible. This is why mobility is so important, as you need to either be able to use distance to retreat to avoid it, or you will have to go forward into the attack to stop it. To be able to effectively stop an attack you will have to develop great stopping power with your tools. This will take a lot of time and hard work. Make sure to put in the effort to hit hard, or you can't make JKD work the way we teach it.

It is also important that you have as much mobility as possible, for the ring or the street. Footwork can be a boring thing to practice, but it forms the foundation of any good fighter. The fighting measure is distance between you and any other person, so you have to train to automatically recognize it, as it will be different between you and another person

When your opponent is right on the edge of the critical distance line, we call it being in the **free fire zone,** sometimes called the **brim of fire.**

Here your opponent passed the critical distance line and being able to touch you.

One way is to maintain the fighting measure is to move back at the same time he moves forward while keeping the fighting measure.

The Fighting Measure:

As he steps forward with his front foot, you quickly step back with your rear foot *(below)*.

Then slide back with your front foot and you are now back at the fighting measure *(below photo)*.

Of course, this will only work if you are able to react in time. This will only happen if you spend the time working on keeping the proper distance between you and your opponent.

It may be that a confrontation in the street will start with a possible opponent right in your face. If he refuses to move back, you must realize quickly that you are not in a good position to defend yourself, so you may have to slide back to the fighting measure.

In a really **c**lose confrontation, you need to step back out of range with your rear foot and return to the fighting measure by sliding back with front foot. punch if you really feel threatened. *(See photo sequence on next page.)*

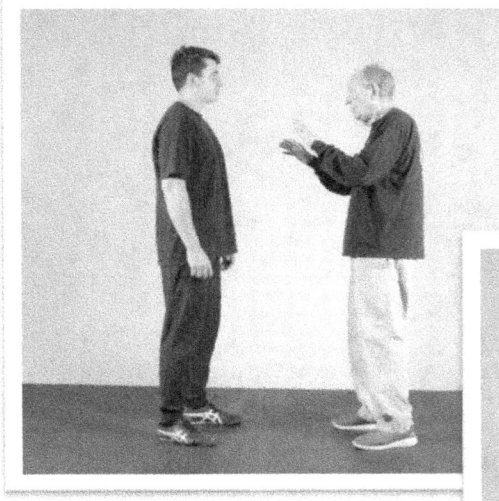

Being present with yourself wherever you may be is at the heart of mindfulness.

As Bruce Lee wrote:

"Avoid mental tenseness, and paralysis by analysis."

Close Confrontation:

You may be able get to safe distance by stepping back with your rear foot at the same time you punch with a front hand horizontal punch *(photos below)*.

Wing Chun Blast to Gain Distance to JKD Blast:

From a close confrontation situation, if you can't step back, you can blast your way to safety. *(See photos below.)*

For almost any straight punch to the head, we aim for the nose for 2 reasons.

1. It is a softer target, so there is less chance of injuring your hand.

2. It can cause enough damage to stop the fight with one powerful punch.

If you have room, you can step forward with your front foot as you strike his chest with snappy palm hit with both palms to gain distance followed by a side kick. *(See photos below and next page.)*

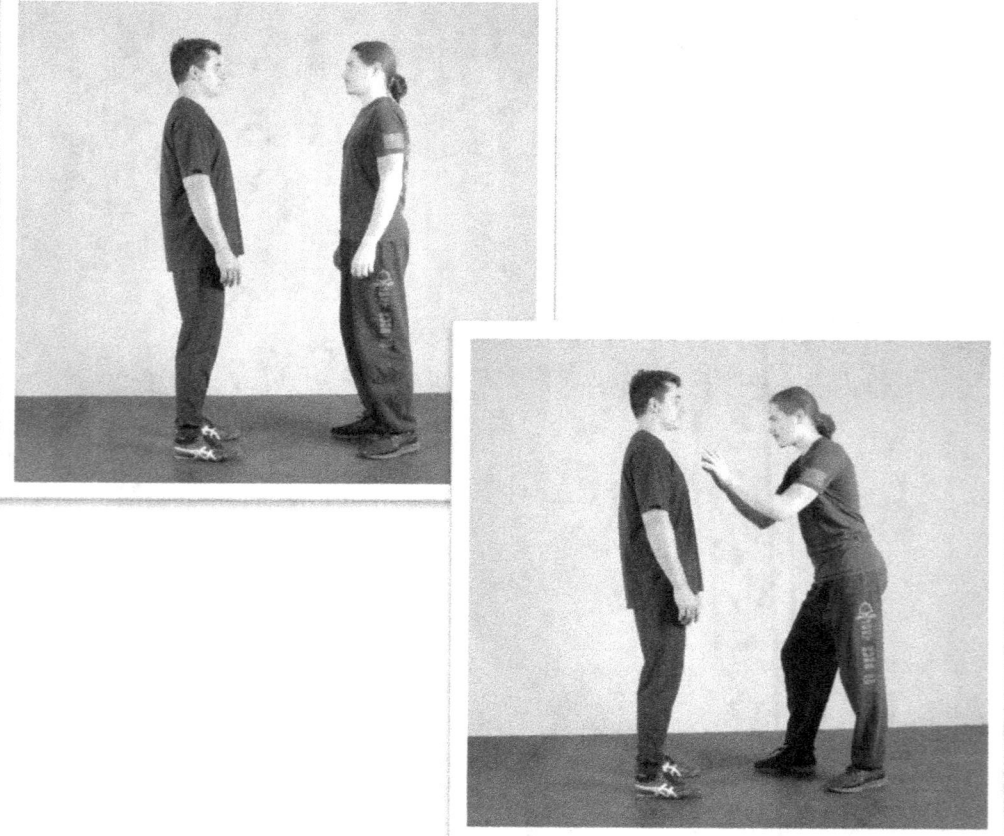

What to do in defending yourself when attacked has 3 basic principles:

1. Get to a position where you are in better position than your opponent

2. Limit the amount of damage that you take

3. Cause as much damage to you opponent as you need to survive.

> *"I call it jeet kune do just because I want to emphasize the notion deciding at the right moment in order to stop the enemy at the gate."*
>
> – BRUCE LEE

I think that some people when they teach JKD choose to ignore the fact that the meaning of Jeet Kune Do is "The Way of the Intercepting fist." One of the reasons might be that intercepting with enough awareness, speed and power is very difficult to master, so they give up on it too soon. Another reason may be that a lot of JKD teachers and students now train with their weak hand forward which makes intercepting with your front hand, which is closer to the target, inefficient as it does not carry as much stopping power as the stronger hand. We try to use the strong front hand to intercept with straight lead punch with enough power to end the fight almost before it started.

Whatever the reason, to really make JKD work you need to put the time in and be able to intercept your opponent's attack. You also need to work on making sure that he cannot intercept your attack. You also need to learn to intercept with sudden explosiveness.

INTERCEPTING

"When your opponent advances, one intercepts."

– BRUCE LEE

Most fighters show some preparation as they attack. In other words, they will telegraph their attack, which gives you an opportunity to counter the attack with a stop hit or kick before the attack reaches its full extension.

In JKD we call this "attack on preparation". We basically think of attacking as our main defense. Bruce Lee called it "offensive defense."

*"To reach me, you must move to me.
Your preparation of attack offers me a directional commitment to intercept you"*

– BRUCE LEE

We divide our defense of the various segments of the attack into the following:

1. Attack on his preparation

2. Attack on delivery (It's on the way)

3. Attack completion, which would be the full extension of his punch or kick

4. Attack on recovery is to strike as the blow is returning to the on-guard position, or as another attack is on the way.

We divide our counter attacks into different units of time called "beats," as follows:

1. When we are attacking on his preparation, we are attacking on his starting to attack. This is the most efficient and the fastest.

2. On his delivery, we are hitting him in the ½ beat

3. On his completion of his attack, we are hitting on the 1 beat

4. On his recovery, we are hitting him on the 1 and ½ beat

Each one is a longer moment of time. The less time your opponent has to attack is better for your chances for victory. Most of these ideas Bruce Lee got from Western fencing.

To make this idea of such an active, rather than a passive defense, really work, you need to be able read your opponent's preparation and to get rid of yours.

At end of the book there is an explanation of the hammer principle drill, which is designed to do both.

When you are training in a class, watch the other students and see if you can pick up on their preparation. Not only is it good practice, but it will give you an advantage when you spar them.

Basic Principles of Intercepting

When he moves forward his forward momentum will add to the power of your interception, as long as you hit him while he is still moving forward.

To be able to intercept you need to be able to:

1. Maintain the fighting measure

2. See the attack coming and be able to distinguish what kind of attack it is.

3. To be able to instantly react with the best tool to stop the attack before it has the time to reach you.

4. We have found that if the attack is on the way, that is slightly easier to stop a kicking attack with a stop hit and a hand attack with a stop kick.

5. The must efficient way to stop an attack is to stop kick on his stepping forward with his lead leg.

Here is one example of training the fighting measure:

The Mirror Drill

The mirror drill is where 2 people are at a fighting measure. One of them will act as a trainer and will move all directions, while the other tries to keep the proper fighting measure distance. Then after a certain time they switch roles.

Fight with strong side forward so that you can make your intercepting really work the way Bruce Lee meant it to work.

Since the great majority of people are right-handed, we are showing it with the right hand forward. If your left hand is strongest hand, then that will be your front hand. We are showing this stance again to stress how essential the principle is.

*"The best way to win a fight is
to just reach over and knock him out."*

– BRUCE LEE to BOB BREMER

The Straight Lead Punch: In many ways the straight lead punch is like Western fencing without the sword. It is the core of JKD. Even though it is the bread and butter of what we teach and really work on applying, it is not something that should be used in all situations. It is the longest punch, and as such should only be used when you are dead certain to be able to hit the target. It is a fully committed punch with the slowest recovery of most hand attacks. It is not a good idea to attack with it, as it can make you vulnerable to a good grappler or boxer. We really only use it in two ways:

1. When we are intercepting and stopping an attack with it.

2. When we use it as a follow up as a finishing blow in a combination attack.

To understand what a straight lead punch is we need to make clear what it is not.

It is not a flicker jab which only use the elbow, and there is no extension of the arm. *(See photos below.)*:

The flicker jab is not a speed jab that extends from the shoulder *(photos below)*.

It is not a power jab that adds the use the hip *(photos below)*.

Each one of these from the time the punch starts, to the hit, and recovery takes a fraction more time the more extension it has, but at the same time, more extension equals more power.

It is a straight lead punch with full body extension *(below)*.

The straight lead consists of three factors:

1. Distance - The punch makes contact at the full extension of the arm.

2. Penetration - To get the maximum power you need to hit the target at end of the punch with a 1-to-2-inch penetration.

3. Snap - The punch ends with a snap at the elbow with a quick recovery.

From Bruce Lee's notes:

The advantages of the straight lead punch:

1. It is faster as the distance between two points is a straight line.

2. It is more accurate, so there is less chance of missing the target than other punches.

3. It can foil an opponent's compound attack when used as a stop hit.

4. It is the most powerful of the straight punches, but you are using more time when you use it.

5. It is used mainly as a stop hit.

From James Lee:

*"If you can get across the first solid blow,
your assailant will be defeated."*

Take What is Offered You.

Every time you are attacked, your opponent will leave an opening. No human being can extend a limb and not leave an opening. You need work on learning how to take advantage of that by taking what the opponent is offering you. Most of the time it seems that people who are proficient in a particular art that has rules, will leave openings that would be considered foul tactics in their art. Even the "no rules" contests have rules. Since many do not practice using these foul tactics, they may not be efficient in defending against them.

This is the whole concept of intercepting. Your opponent attacks, and you take advantage of the opening he gives you by intercepting and stopping his attack. This is why we work so much on hitting him with a side kick to the knee as soon he steps forward with enough power to break his leg, as that is the easiest and most efficient way to stop an attack.

Examples:

Intercepting with a shin/knee kick as your opponent steps toward you. *(See photos next page).*

Intercepting on his step forward with a leg obstruction to a trap and hit *(below)*.

From a natural stance you intercept as he steps forward with a hook *(below)*.

CLOSE RANGE DEFENSE

Although close range attacks happen, they are not something that you will want to happen. This is why it is important to keep up your awareness at all time but you can sometimes be attacked by surprise. You need to react quickly before any hold is too tight. I realize that is much easier said than it is to do it.

He starts to grab her *(below)*:

He is "offering" her his eyes. She takes advantage of it with a double thumb strike to his eyes *(below)*:

She takes advantage of the handle his ponytail gives her by grabbing it and pulling at the same time she grabs his chin. She then throws him to the ground by twisting his head and stepping back with her rear foot *(below)*.

Bert Poe called grabbing The ponytail, "using the handle." Watch for any "handle" your Opponent may offer you.

She then stomps on his face.

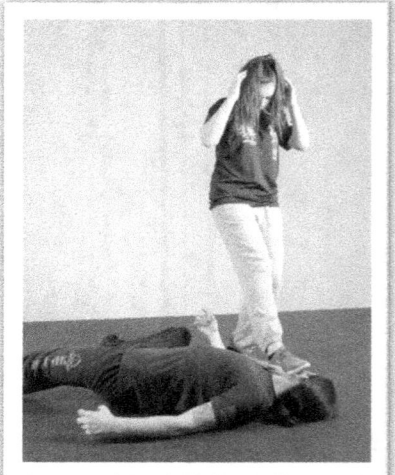

Sometimes you are taken by surprise and are attacked when your opponent is already too close to you, as in a crowded environment. This is why you need to train some close-range fighting. Even if most of your training is as a stand-up fighter, you will need to be able survive a close-range attack, which is also called "within arm's reach". It is a good idea to:

1. Study some of the World War II close combat techniques.

2. Learn some grappling like judo, catch wrestling or Brazilian jiu jitsu.

3. Work on staying or your feet and getting back on your feet as quickly as you can. You can spend time on the ground in the ring, but in the street, it is always best to stay on your feet.

Our late friend Bert Poe was a great close range combative instructor. He told us that when you are fighting on the ground, to just break something and get back on your feet.

"At Close Range" Examples:

Although at very close range your opponent does not offer as many targets as he does in the above examples, there are still a few that you can get to.

Tight Front Hug

She grabs his chin and shoves forward bending him back and off balance. She then knees him in the groin as she steps forward which throws him to the ground *(below)*.

Here she is grabbed from the front with her arms inside. She slaps and grabs his groin and pulls as if starting a lawn mower:

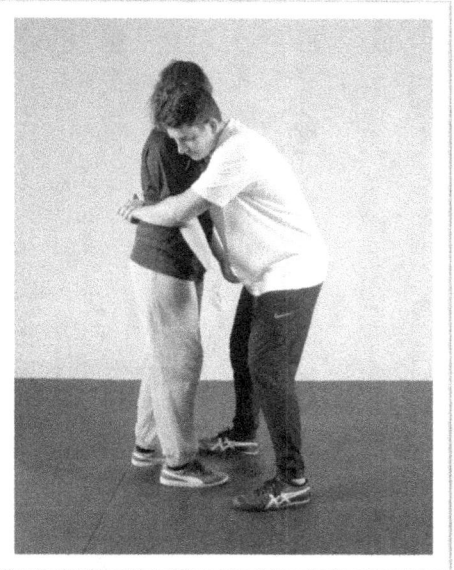
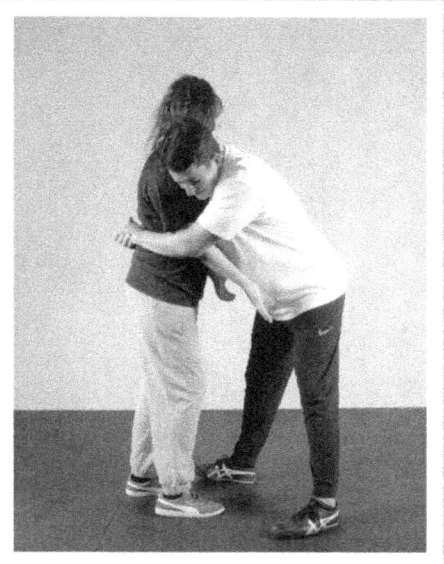

This should make him let go of her. She then knees him in the groin and shoves him to the ground as she steps forward:

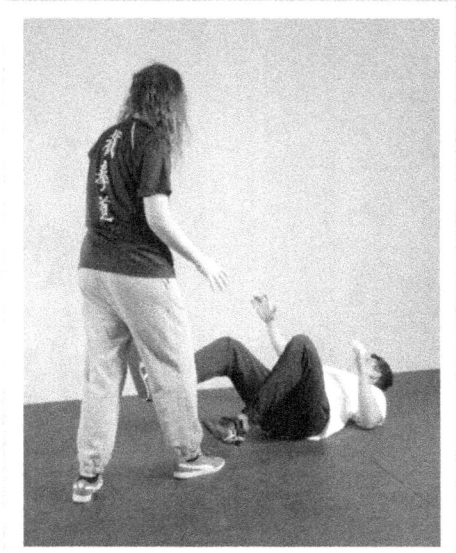

Here she is grabbed from behind with her arms inside. She gets some space by taking a deep breath while raising her arms. This gives her enough room to step back while slapping his groin:

She then straightens his arm and locks it. She then throws him to the ground, as she steps back with her front leg. Then she finishes him with a stomp to his head *(below)*.

Grabbed from behind with her arms on the outside. She twists her body and steps out with her left foot. This gives her enough room to attack the groin:

When he reacts to the groin hit, she locks his arm. She then steps back with her right leg and shoves him to the ground. She then finishes him off with a stomp kick to his head.

You opponent has gotten you in a rear naked choke. If you are taken off balance as the strangle is applied, it's pretty much lights out. If you can, you *may* be able to give yourself some room by violently twisting clockwise by stepping out with your left leg as you lift up on his elbow while hitting his groin. Then twist so you face him and shove him back by pushing hard on his chin. You can then follow-up with a knee to the groin. You can then take him to the ground by stepping down while shoving his head towards the floor. *(See sequence below and on next page.)*

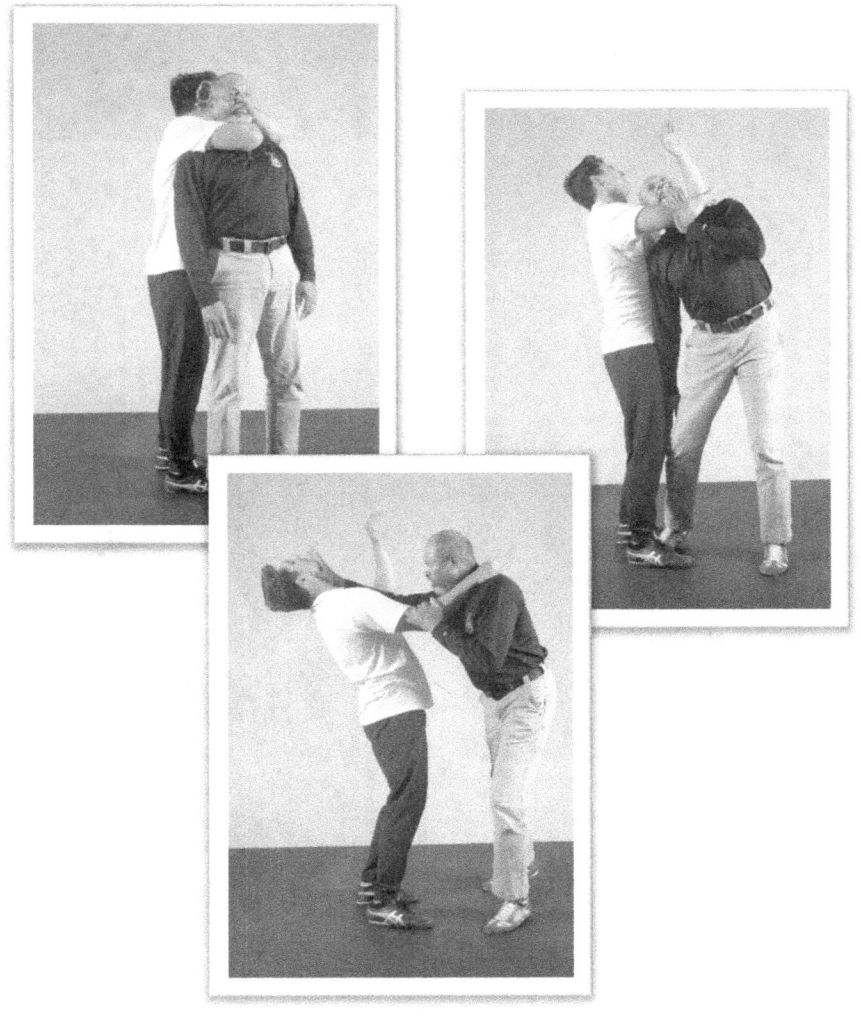

As he steps forward to grab you, grab his chin with your left hand as you push his face back your fingers in his eyes *(below)*.

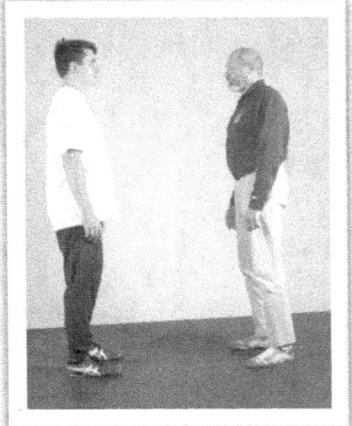

Twist his head, then elbow it. Follow by a knee to his head. You can also go to an elbow attack, followed by another knee to the face.

Step down as you shove him to the ground *(below)*.

"Avoid long battles – win and win quickly."
from *The Art of War* by SUN TZU

The longer a fight goes on the more danger a defender is in. Work on focusing on gaining power in your tools for striking, timing your counter-attack, hitting to where it will do the most damage, and in the shortest time possible.

MOBILITY AND STILLNESS

"Footwork can beat any attack, and a properly maintained distance will baffle any skilled opponent."

– BRUCE LEE

Mobility: The purpose of mobility is to avoid the attack or respond with your tools as quickly as possible and end the attack. When practicing footwork vary the length and/or the speed of your steps.

Mobility in Defense: It is very important to work on mobility as a large part of your defensive strategy. Your defensive mobility does not have to be large movements. Below are just a few examples:

As the attacker starts to attack, the defender angles right and kicks to an open target. *(See photos below and on next page.)*

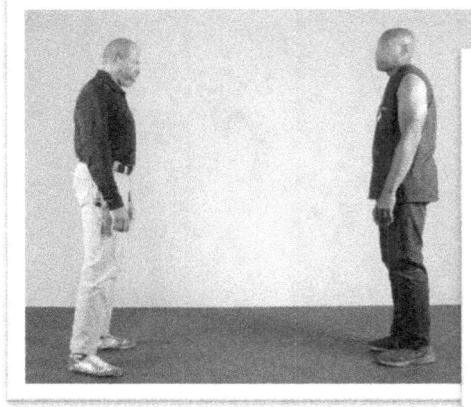

As the opponent steps to hit, the defender steps to the right and intercepts with a straight lead punch. The footwork should be done as one unit of time, that is as one action *(below)*.

As the attacker attempts a rear round kick, The defender steps forward and to the left, and scores with straight left stop hit *(below)*.

As the opponent tries to score with a straight rear punch, the defender slips inside with his own straight rear punch used as a stop hit. The technique would be exactly the same against a right jab *(below)*.

As the attacker slides up and side kicks, the defender moves back just enough to avoid contact and scores with a straight lead as the attacker's foot touches the ground *(below)*.

Mobility in Attack: Work on the many different ways you can use footwork to deliver an attack like the side kick. Having good use of mobility in an attack can ensure that you hit your opponent right where you want to, and at the correct distance for maximum power.

Examples: (See next page.)

The attacker attempts to hit with a right punch. The defender moves back to avoid the punch. The attacker, to gain distance, slides his rear foot and steps forward and hits with a right punch *(below)*.

When we use footwork this way, it disguises the distance we can get. We call this type of footwork *"cheating the distance."*

Close up photos of the footwork:

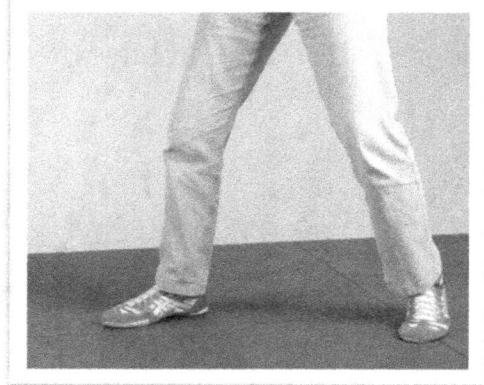
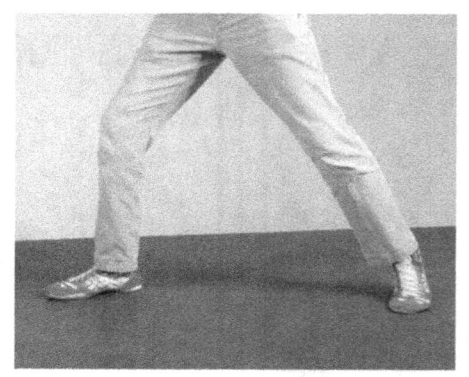
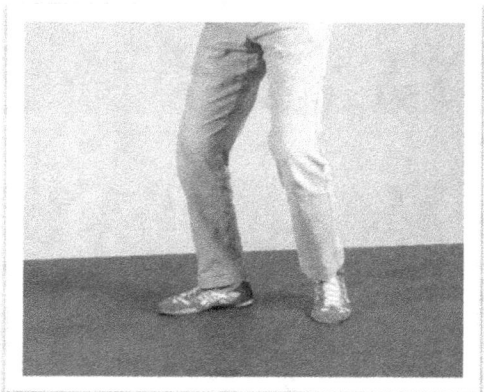
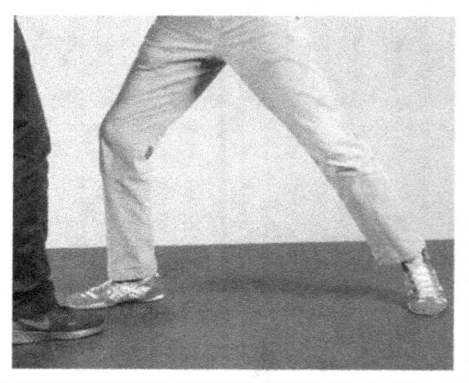

When using a slide side kick, you slide your rear foot up to gain distance for your side kick. The rear leg is the measuring stick for the side kick. Because the distance between you and your opponent is seldom the same distance, how far you slide the rear foot up never exactly the same. Make sure you train it that way. *(See photo sequence on next page.)*

Curve right as you punch. This will put you in a better position for your attack because you are angling away from his counter-attacking tools *(below)*.

Stillness in Mind and Body

> *"Can you look at something without naming it?*
> *Naming it, making it a word, causes fear."*
>
> – BRUCE LEE

One of the hardest things to do when you are confronted with a situation that can lead to violence is to maintain your composure.

You need to train working under stress, while keeping focused on the task at hand. While there is no way to really prepare for sudden violence in a classroom setting, for the simple reason that the student knows that he is in a safe environment. There are some drills however that may help a student deal with a real self-defense situation. What Bruce Lee is talking about is Mushin which is the Zen concept of "no mind", or freedom from distracting thoughts. The more relaxed and calm you are the more you can react quickly and violently to whatever happens. At the same time, you also need be aware of your environment and the other people who may be present. Being present with yourself wherever you may be is at the heart of mindfulness

An excellent resource to train for real world violence is the series of books on violence by Rory Miller.

Stress Training Drills:

1. At fighting measure, have one student yell, scream and threaten. Then have him suddenly attack. The student then stop hits or kicks.

2. A 2- or 3-on-1 sparring session

3. The ½ circle drill - Three students are in front of a student while the trainer is behind him. All four are

wearing boxing gloves. When the trainer points to one of the three, he will attack with a flurry of fast punches that are heavy but not hard enough to really injure the student. At first the student may react by turning his back to the attack. If possible don't let the student know what is going to happen.

4. Your idea

Work on your reaction to an attack from stillness of mind to explosive response. There will be a reactionary gap between the awareness that something is happening and the moment we take action. You can shorten that gap by how you train and how much effort you put into your training.

Some Examples:

As the attacker steps forward, the defender checks his advance. He then steps down hard with his front foot as he hits his attacker. *(See photos below.)*

As the attacker starts to throw wide hook, the defender lowers his body and delivers a body blow which allows him to explode with a powerful straight lead as a follow-up attack *(below)*.

Adaptability: Learning to "Fit in"

Relationship - What Bruce Lee meant by this is that to do a technique you need to study, as Bruce Lee wrote, "oneself in action *with* the opponent", which he called fitting in.

Combat is never static, but ever changing. You need to be able to deal with any stimulus with the proper response. To do this you need to fit in with what is happening at every moment. Learn to adapt to whatever is on front of you.

For example, if he is advancing, you might retreat to keep the fighting measure, or you may advance with stop hit or kick, depending on the opponent and/or circumstances.

PRINCIPLES OF ATTACK

"You may be able learn the mechanics of an attack with some effort, but to apply a tool against a moving opponent with exact timing, and to the precise area to do the most damage, and at the correct distance takes a lot of practice. Too many students concentrate on practicing a technique, but never really work in applying it in in a combat situation."

– From *Principles of Attack,* by JAMES LEE

Sifu James Lee ran Bruce Lee's Oakland school. He said the first principle of attack is *courage,* the second is *power,* and the third is *technique*.

In his teachings, Lee advised:

1. Avoid his strength and attack his weakness
2. When you see an opening advance and attack ceaselessly
3. Defeat or victory lies in your speed and power

We teach that there are 7 factors in an attack:

1. A fine sense of timing
2. A perfect judgement of distance
3. Enough speed to score a hit
4. Enough power to end the fight

5. Attacking with confidence

6. Attacking with accuracy

7. And don't attack where your opponent is, but rather where he will be.

The 5 Ways of Attack

Bruce Lee taught that there were five basic ways to attack someone. There were many reasons he did this. Some of them are as follows:

1. To be able to put each one in a separate category as a way to analyze each one.

2. To study which is the most efficient and which is the least.

3. To figure out which one would work best on what type of opponent.

4. To understand what type of opponent that category of attack would be of little value, or not advised to use against because it could be too easily countered.

5. To understand that not all are equal in value against all types of fighters.

6. Not to be bound to any one way to one attack.

The 5 Ways Are:

1A. Single Direct Attack (SDA)

This is a single attack that goes directly to the target. It requires speed and accuracy to work.

1B. Single Angular Attack (SAA)

This is the same as an SDA attack except that your attack comes in at an angle.

2A. Attack By Combination (ABC)

This is a series of attacks in sequence. For example: jab-cross-hook in boxing, or a backfist to a side kick in kickboxing

2B. Attack by combination with broken rhythm (ABCWBR)

This is when you pause after one of your hits to break the rhythm of your attack in order to fool his defensive response

3. Progressive Indirect Attack (PIA)

This is a feint to one line to create an open line for your attack to score. This works on someone who uses distance or blocking as defense. But this form of attack should not work on anyone who knows JKD and focuses on intercepting. As soon as he sees a fake or a feint, he should react with a stop hit or kick before your opponent has finished his feint.

4. Hand Immobilization Attack (HIA)

This is also called a hair, hand and leg immobilization attack. This is the trapping hands aspect of JKD where you immobilize one or more of your opponent's limbs.

5. Attack by Drawing (ABD)

This is when you want the opponent to attack by leaving a part of your body open so your opponent will attack it, and you can counterattack. With ABD done right and without being too obvious, you can almost be certain where your opponent will attack, and you will be able to score with a counter-attack.

Remember these ways of attack are not meant to work on every opponent, as some only work best on certain types of fighters. Make sure to try all ways in practice and see what works best for you.

Some of the Functions of an Attack:

    1. To move ahead of the opponent's defense

    2. To put him on the defensive

    3. To control timing and distance

The Safest Way to Enter is with a Kick, or a Jam, or a Shield.

Examples:

Entering with Side Kick to a Finger Jab.
(See photos on next page.)

Entering with hook kick to hammer back fist *(below):*

Entering with a leg obstruction to a downward hammer fist strike *(below):*

Entering with a jam to a straight lead punch *(below)*.

This is called the shield entry as your front leg acts as a shield to cover some of your body as you enter. As you slide up with a shield entry, trap his front arm. As you come down trap both his arms as you hit *(below)*.

Directness is to attack in a direct line from point A to point B on the straightest path possible, which is also the fastest route to the target.

> *"Directness is when every everything is stripped down to the essential."*
>
> – BRUCE LEE

For example, from your fist to his nose on a straight line.

When a reporter asked Bruce Lee what Jeet Kune Do was, he took his wallet and tossed it to him. The reporter caught it. Bruce told him that was JKD, as **t**he reporter just caught it naturally. He did not jump into a stance. He just reacted simply and directly.

Two Examples:

The JKD Groin Kick

The direct finger jab to eye *(below)*:

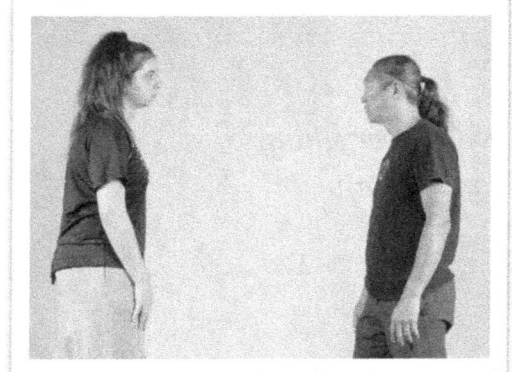
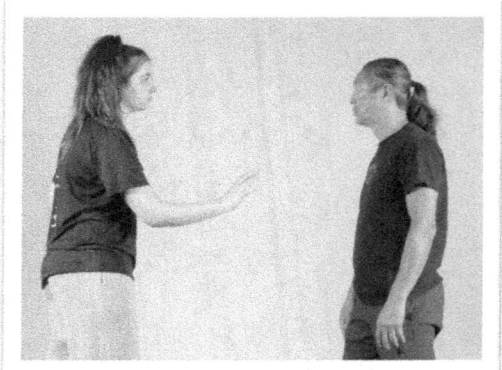
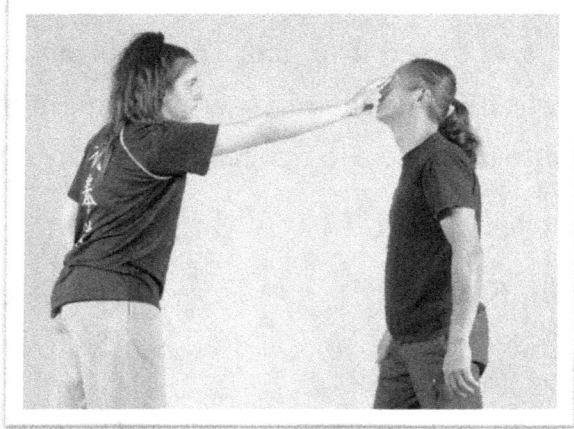

Simplicity

*"The height of cultivation is nothing special.
It is mere simplicity, the ability to express the utmost
with the minimum. It is the halfway cultivation that
leads to ornamentation."*

– BRUCE LEE

When training look for the simplest response to a stimulus, if possible.

"If someone grabs you, punch them."

– BRUCE LEE

A simple thumb strike will work to make him let go *(below)*.

Grab him and pull down hitting him twice in the eyes. Then roll him over, and hit him in the eyes once more, as she starts to get up and leave. *(See photos on next page.)*

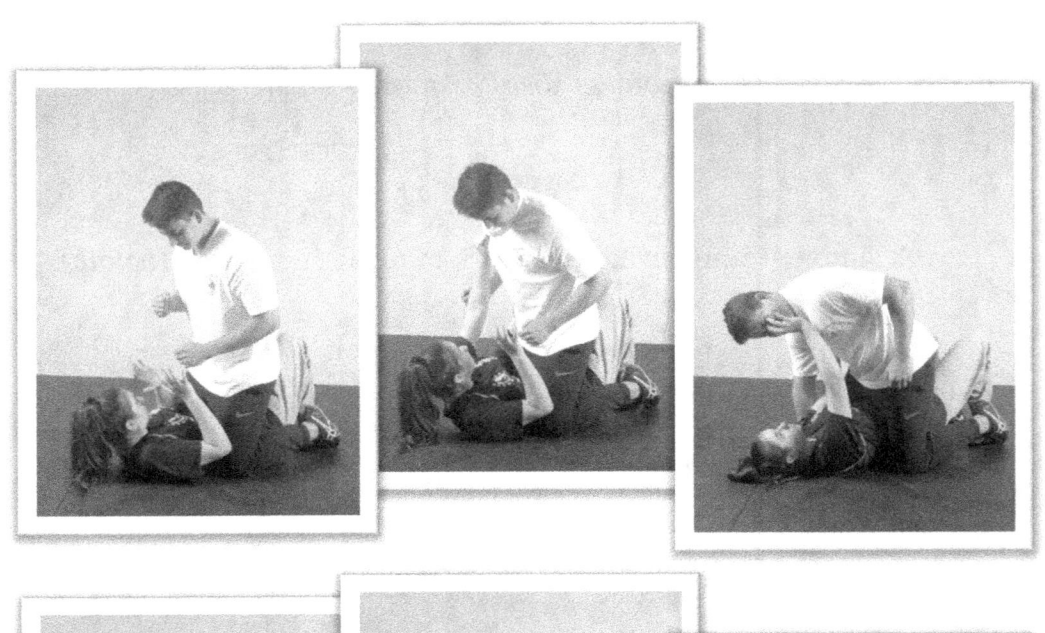
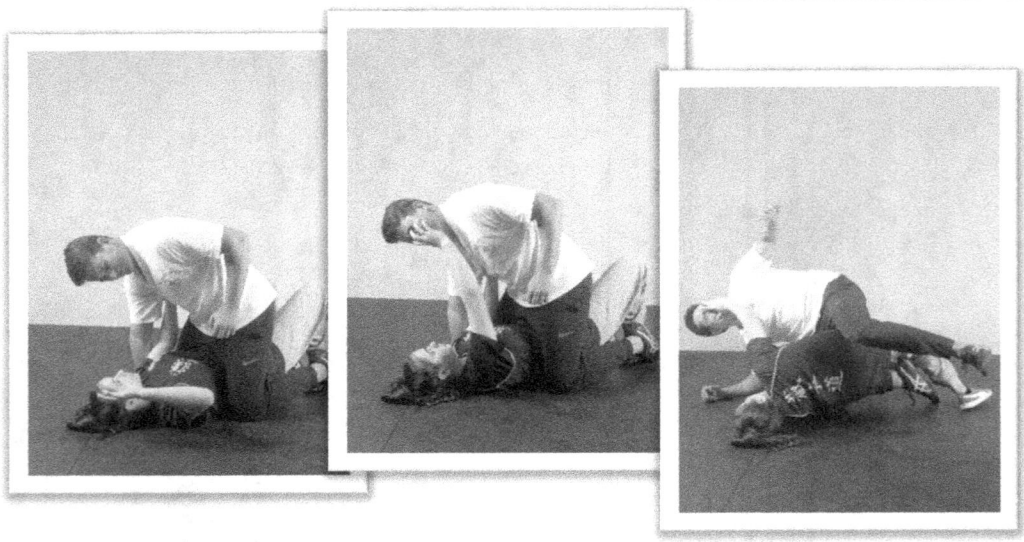

Double heavy palm strike to ears to double thumb strike to eyes *(below)*.

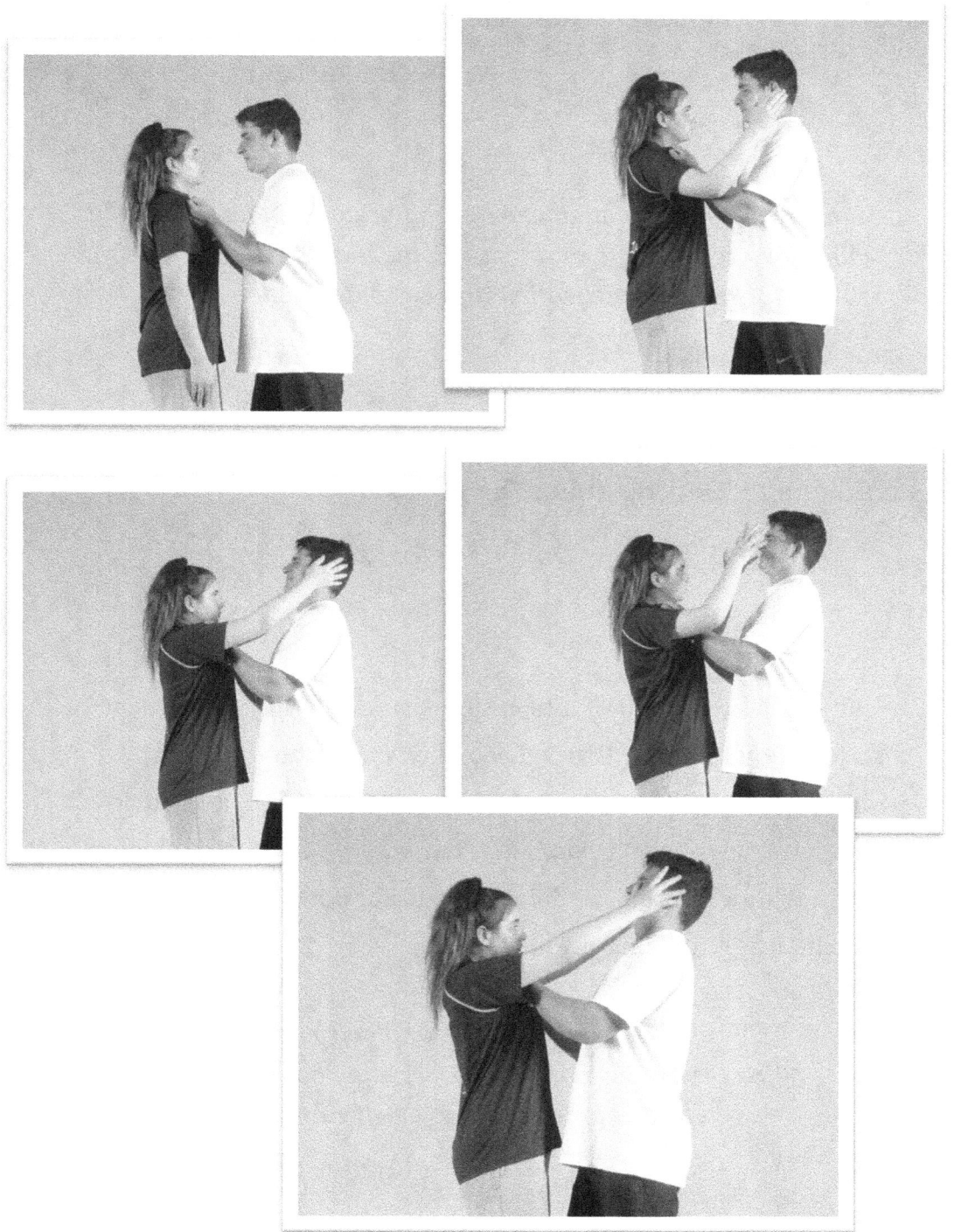

"It is indeed difficult to see the situation simply – our minds are very complex – and it is easy to teach one to be skillful, but it is difficult to teach him his own attitude."

– BRUCE LEE

"Simplicity is 'daily minimize instead of daily increase.' Being wise does not mean to add more. Being wise means be able to get off sophistication and be simply simple."

– BRUCE LEE

Efficiency – Getting rid of the clicks

"Efficiency is anything that scores."

– BRUCE LEE

If you take a video of a technique, what it really consists of is a series of still photos. Bruce Lee called each photo a "click". In a technique, or a series of techniques, the main idea is to get rid of as many of the clicks a possible. That way you will be achieving efficiency in what you are doing by cutting down on the time you are committing to doing it.

"I refer to my hands, feet and body as tools of the trade. The hands and feet must be sharpened and improve daily to be efficient."

– BRUCE LEE

What you are trying to do is trap is blocking hand and hit him, but it takes too many clicks *(below)*.

This way does the same thing but takes less time. The last 2 photos are really one motion as you jerk his arm down at the same time you hit him with a palm hook *(below)*.

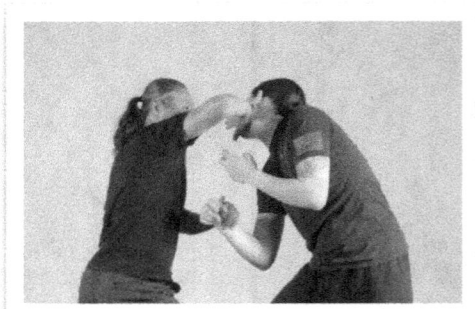

You punch. He blocks. You trap and hit.

We see this all the time. The problem is that we don't really punch like that. If you are punching and leaving your arm out there, you need to rethink how and why you are punching.

The whole idea of how we teach trapping is that we trap on his punch or after a leg obstruction. This sequence requires two movements. *(See photos top of next page.)*

When he punches you simply cut into the tool and pak at the same time. It becomes one movement (below).

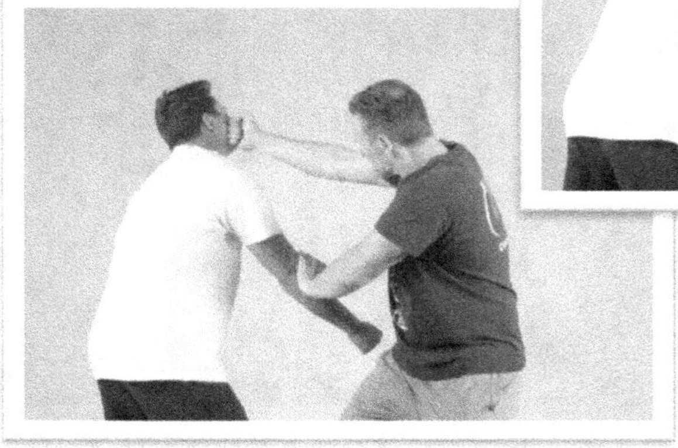

He punches. You parry and hit (below).

He punches. You both trap and hit him at the same time with a sliding leverage finger jab.

THE TIME COMMITMENT THEORY

The more time you take to do something the more time your opponent has to counter you.

Understanding the Time Commitment Theory will help you further understand:

The difference between snappy and heavy hitting.

When you do a snappy punch or kick, it takes less time to recover than heavy kick. When you do a proper straight lead punch, your punch should land at full extension with a one-to-two-inch penetration. This should give you a quick recovery or follow-up attack. A snappy punch or kick relies on speed and snap for power in its delivery system.

A heavy punch or kick relies less on speed and more on hitting through the target with weight. Take, for example, the difference in recovery between Thai round kick and a Savate round kick. The Thai kick while having more power commits more time from attack to recovery than a Savate kick. The Savate, while having less power, is a faster kick from the start of the kick to its recovery. It is the same for the difference between jab in boxing and a heavy hsing-I heavy palm strike.

Understanding the difference in combat is important.

In a combination attack, it may be a good idea for the first hit to be a snappy one to hurt him without overcommitting. Then follow up with a heavy one to finish him. You may not want to just attack with a heavy punch or kick unless you are sure you will hit your target.

When Bob Bremer first saw the rear leg round Thai kick in person, he told us that it was a great and powerful kick. He went on to add that because of the Thai stance, with its rear leg closer than the rear leg is in our JKD stance, it is efficient and fast, but to attempt if from our stance would take more time to land the kick. Then he said we should not attack with it, but rather use it to finish an opponent.

While blocking and parrying for defense is sometimes necessary, it is not ideal.

Anytime you block or parry a punch, there is lag in time between the punch and the return hit. Your opponent may be able to take advantage of the time between the block and your hit, by striking you after the block but before the hit. This is especially true if you block an opponent's feint and then try to hit.

While a simultaneous block and hit or a sliding leverage hit is better than a block and then a hit, to intercept his attack is still the best way to control time.

Some tools take more time than others. This is why you need to be aware of the time between your techniques in combination attack.

Learn to hurt him with a flick.

Some of the time a loose, snappy and fast attack like a finger slice to the eye can end a fight with little effort on your part

Fighting Measure -- Front Hand Too Low

When the front hand is too low, the finger slice will score. This is also example of, "Take what is offered you." It is like snapping a whip. *(See photos next page.)*

The snappy inverted hook kick to the groin. The last photo shows the snap back of the kick. *(See photos below and next page.)*

The Longest Weapon Against the Closest Target

This the most simple, direct, and efficient method of attack, and one of the foundational principles of Jeet Kune Do.

The Shin Knee Side Kick

The Finger Jab

FEINTING AND FAKING
(FALSE ATTACKS)

A fake is when a JKD practitioner uses one of his limbs to distract his opponent from his true line of attack. Basically, it is an incomplete attack that deceives the opponent and opens a line.

A delayed hit is a false attack and is different from a feint, as it is intended to fall short so the opponent will try and block it. This will leave an opening, so the attacker can score a hit by finishing his attack to another line.

A feint is an offensive action aimed at diverting the opponent's attention from the real point of attack. A good feint should look like a real attack.

A good feint should so believable that it forces the opponent react to it, so that he leaves an opening for your real attack.

Some examples of these attacks are:

1. High feint to low hit
2. Low feint to high hit
3. Feint to the high inside line to hit to the high outside line
4. Feint to the high outside line to hit to the high inside line

Feint a low front hand attack to draw the parry. Then trap his front arm to a hammer fist *(below)*.

Feint a low straight punch. This time he attempts to parry with his rear hand, and you trap the front hand as you strike with a heavy palm hit.

A good way to train this is after you work on both of the above false attacks, is to have students practice where one does the feint while the other either tries to parry either his front or rear hand. The other student will react with the proper technique. This makes the drill a little more alive, as the one attacking has to react to what the defender is offering. You are trying to automatically attack the line that is opening. Try to do this way to train as many ways as possible with other techniques.

Feint a high finger jab to draw a front hand block to a straight rear punch *(below)*.

Feint a low kick to draw a front hand block followed by a high straight lead punch. *(See photos on next page.)*

Feint a high finger jab on the outside line. As he starts to parry with his front hand, do a small circle disengagement to a finger jab to the inside line while checking his front arm. *(See photo sequence on next page.)*

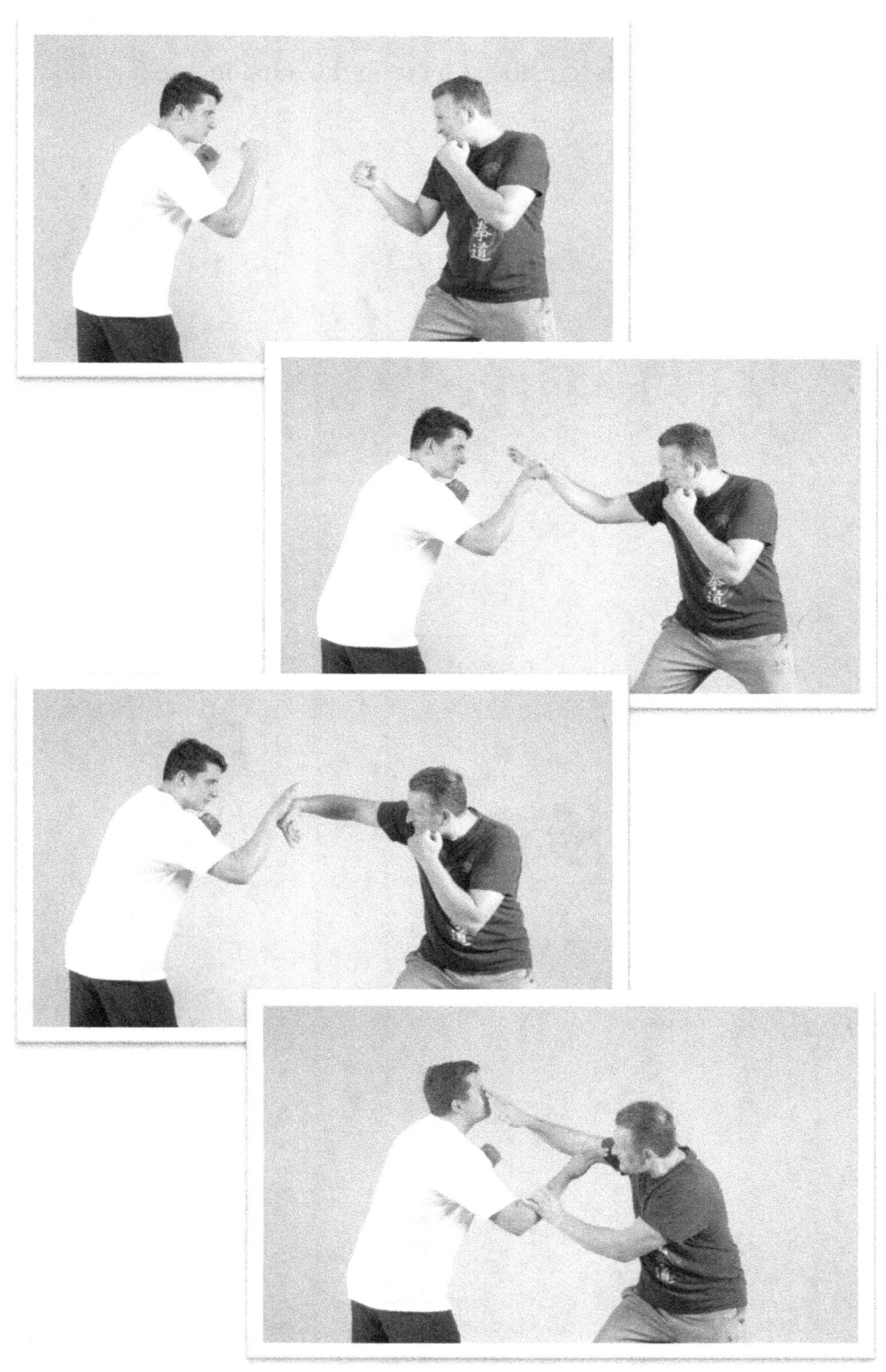

Feint a hit to the high inside to a hit on the outside line *(below)*.

The Delayed Hit:

You feint a hit to the high inside line to get a reaction, and you see that he parries with his front hand *(below)*.

This time you start to hit and then stop. You then continue the hit on the outside line, as over parries, leaving the outside line open.

One of the problems some JKD students have is thinking that a false attack will work on someone who understands JKD. It shouldn't because as soon as he starts to feint or fake, he should be intercepted. Never try to parry or block unless you are taken by surprise.

He feints a low attack and is met with stop kick *(below)*.

He either feints or fake a kick. It doesn't matter what he does because as soon as he starts his kick, you hit him *(below)*.

It really doesn't matter if he steps forward to hit, kick, feint or fake. You just stop him with a leg obstruction, or a stop hit.

He steps forward to attack and is stopped with a stop hit *(below)*.

This time it's a leg obstruction used to stop a back fist attack *(below)*.

He tries to attack with a front kick and is stopped with the leg obstruction *(below)*.

The leg obstruction used against a rear round kick *(below)*.

From a Natural Stance:

As he steps toward the defender simply uses a leg obstruction *(below)*.

We have found that the leg obstruction is one of our most useful tools for many reasons. The number one reason is just how versatile it is.

1. You can attack with it, which will stop his stop hit or kick.

2. You can use it against almost any attack.

3. From the leg obstruction it is the easiest way to follow up with a trap and hit or a straight blast.

4. Sometimes even with a kick.

5. It can be done from either an on-guard or natural stance.

The first time I went to train Jeet Kune Do was at Dan Inosanto's backyard school. The last half hour of class we did some sparring. The first person I sparred against was Bob Bremer. As soon as I stepped forward, he moved in and intercepted me with a perfect leg obstruction. I could not move either forward or backwards. Bob just grinned at me. After about 20 seconds he dropped down and gently tapped me on the top of my head with his boxing glove.

Bob was the first one I ever saw using it. In fact, he was the only one I ever saw do it. The first time I saw it in print was in "Jeet Kune Do", a book of Bruce Lee's notes, that were not in the "Tao of Jeet Kune Do". It was put together and edited by John Little. In the book there are some of Bruce's lesson plans. In one of the first lesson plans is the leg obstruction.

The hammer principle was also listed in the lesson plans. Bob Bremer had us work on both the leg obstruction and the hammer principle soon after he started coming to my garage class every Wednesday night. They both became a big part of our training. The hammer principle will be explained later in this book.

RHYTHM AND BROKEN RHYTHM

It's very hard for a fixed type of defense to fit in with broken rhythm as most people train to attack in a steady rhythm, and most of their defense training is usually against a steady rhythm.

Rhythm either be steady or broken.

1-2: This is a steady beat – It is like a jab – cross in boxing, or a Back fist followed by a kick in kick boxing

- 1-2: The "negative one-two" is a fake or feint followed by a positive hit.

O.n.e - 2: This one is difficult to explain in words or even still photos. I had never seen or heard of this until I read the book of Bruce Lee's notes on attack edited by John Little. On the ways of attack, Bruce wrote 1-2 followed by O.n.e - 2.

Once I said the O.n.e slower than the 2 I figured out that the O.n.e - 2 was at a different rhythm than the 1-2.

This is how it works:

For example, if you throw a snappy finger slice to an opponent's eye followed by a rear finger jab, you cannot hit with the rear finger jab until the finger slice snaps back.

But if you throw the finger jab slower and heaver to and still use full extension to the eye (o.n.e.) followed by a rear finger jab to the eye, the time between the 2 hits is faster than the 1-2 hits. By doing this and still using a full extension to the eye followed by a finger jab to the eye, the time between the 2 hits is faster than the 1-2 hits. By doing this it is easy to score a hit. If he doesn't block the finger slice, he will get hit in the eye. If he does block it, he will get hit with the rear finger jab. This is both hard to do and understand.

1-2-3: This is steady rhythm

1- 2 -3: This is broken rhythm Hit – hit – pause hit

1- 2-3: Hit – pause – hit – hit

Bruce Lee wrote that a fighter could cut down an opponent's movement time by either disturbing his rhythm, immobilizing him, forcing him to provide an initial reaction, which could be acted upon, and by avoiding or deflecting his movement.

The jab, cross, hook from boxing as an example of broken rhythm *(below):*

1. If the Speed of the jab, cross, hook is steady with no pause between the punches, the rhythm is steady

2. If you pause after jab and before the cross, or after the cross and before the hook, you are breaking the rhythm

   a. Jab and pause, cross, hook

   b. Jab, cross and pause, hook

Try practicing broken rhythm in all your drills. A good way to start is do the above rhythms on the focus gloves.

ECONOMY OF MOTION

"In kicking and striking, especially from the ready stance, eliminate all unnecessary motions and muscle contractions which slow and fatigue you without accomplishing any useful purpose." Bruce Lee

Try to stay as loose and relaxed as possible. Make every motion count, and work on getting maximum results with a minimum of energy. You can learn a lot about this principle by discussing the cleanest, shortest attacks possible in any situation with your teacher and fellow students. Understanding the economy of motion is important for any art, as it can give you an advantage in any fight.

"My technique is the result of your technique."
– BRUCE LEE

If you are defending against an attack, attacking, or counter-attacking, what you do will depend on what your opponent does.

For example: If you attack and he retreats, you can continue your attack, pause, or retreat. In any case, in combat you can never be sure what your opponent will do. You need to train with this in mind, by training for it. Too much training is based on the following:

1. I do this technique

2. Then you do this technique

3. Then I will do this technique

4. And so on.

Combat is never fixed. It is ever changing, and your training must be "alive" and not "dead". You must be able to flow with what is happening at the moment it is happening. If you are doing stimulus and response training always with a same response, you need to move on to more advanced training.

One of the best ways to do this is practice an attack and when your partner blocks it, you respond to it with a follow-up response. Once you have mastered this single response, add a different response. For example: the response may be that:

1. He blocks with his front hand

2. He blocks with his rear hand

3. He uses distance to avoid the attack

4. He shoots in for a take down

Once you have worked one response, add another. Next time when you punch, he can do either # 1 or 2 above or any combination until you are just reacting to what is happening without thought. Try not to have any preconceived idea of what action you partner will do. Just learn to flow with whatever is happening at that moment in time

What all this really means is that simplicity is the best way to react to a given response. While you need to practice this type of training, intercepting is still the best method of defense.

Leg Obstruction Followed by a Punch

The above sequence is both simple and direct. The following sequence is direct, but not too simple to do.

THE 3 STAGES OF COMBAT

I have seen two different plaques on the 3 stages of combat in Jeet Kune Do.

One is:

1. **Partiality** - Sharpening the tool
2. **Fluidity** - Utilizing the tool
3. **Emptiness** - Dissolving the tool

The other is:

1. Sticking to the nucleus
2. Liberation from nucleus
3. Returning to original freedom

What it All Means is This:

When you start taking martial arts you do not "know what a punch or kick is". As you are learning, you are introduced to many punches and kicks. You learn how and when to do all the things you are learning. You practice many ways to get your punches and kicks better and better. After a while "a punch is not longer just a punch, and a kick is no longer just a kick". One day you find yourself just reacting to what is in front of you without thought. It's as if you don't punch "it" punches. After this you have returned to your "original freedom" and "a punch is just a punch, and a kick is just a kick".

When you are walking down the street and as bird flies at your head, you don't think "There's a bird flying at my head, so I must duck". If you are driving down a street and a child runs in front of your car, you simply slam on your brakes. You just react without thought. This reaction is built into the human brain to help you survive. This is how you must instantly react to any punch or kick coming at you, as there is no time to think about it. This is how we try and teach the principle of intercepting.

There's a good story that illustrates the idea of original freedom:

There once was a young man who touched a hot stove and quickly reacted by quickly moving hand off of the stove. When his friend asked him how he did it, he said he didn't know; he just did it.

His friend said that was the problem because he had never learned the proper method of taking his hand off of a hot stove, he could have been hurt. His friend told him that he knew a master of taking your hand off a hot stove. The master taught him a method where you moved it off by moving up and forward. He practiced for a year on a cold stove. He then found another master with a different way. Then he found another one then another and another one. Until he knew 7 different methods of taking your hand off a hot stove which he practiced every day on a cold stove, until he accidently touched a hot stove and was severely burned.

"Real combat is not fixed, and it is very much alive."

– BRUCE LEE

PRINCIPLES OF DEFENSE

In reality, defense is anything which opposes an attack. It is a way of preventing an attack.

Avoid passive moves. No passive defense.

A passive move is when you parry or block an attack. You need to try and avoid them as passive move gives more time for your opponent to react.

A fake or feint can beat a passive defense. First you throw a jab, and he parries it with his rear hand *(below)*.

If you then start the same punch then stop it (the delayed hit), when he parries it, you can now hit to the open line. *(See photos on next page.)*

It is sometimes difficult to show some things with still photos. By his parrying, his attacker knew that he could score a hit, by faking to draw the parry, and then hitting to the now open line.

If you must parry because you are taken by surprise, make sure to intercept the next attack if possible.

Broken rhythm in defense is upsetting you opponent's attacking rhythm. You do this by hitting between his beats of his attack.

The trainer throws a jab to a cross from Western boxing. The student catches the jab and does a shoulder roll against the cross. *(See below.)*

While the catch and the shoulder roll are passive moves, they are taught and practiced, because you can't always be able to intercept. Sometimes you need to roll with the punches. These moves are important for beginning students when the are learning to spar. It can instill confidence and cut down on injuries.

This time after catching the jab he intercepts the cross with his front hand. He breaks attacker's rhythm by intercepting on the 1 and ½ beat *(below)*.

Punch when you have to punch and kick when you have to kick. Don't stop to think about it. Just automatically do what you need to do at the time you are doing it.

Close range to scoop kick. Followed by a back fist *(below)*.

Close range to punch as soon as the attacker starts to hit. This is using the wing chun principle of "thrusting forward when the is freed" *(below)*.

The Principles of Fighting More Than One Opponent

1. Quickly finish the leader first
2. Attack to the side and use one of them as a shield
3. When close use hands in combination
4. When in kicking distance use kicking combinations

TRAINING METHODS

One must be free. Free to change a drill if it didn't fit the requirements, free to adapt. If a drill doesn't work throw it away but work on trying to get it first.

*"Knowing is not enough we; we must apply.
Willing is not enough we must do."*

— BRUCE LEE

From my JKD notes from my Sifu Dan Inosanto:

Training Process Model

1. **Knowledge** - The remembering of previously learned material.

2. **Comprehension** - The ability to grasp the meaning of the material.

3. **Application** - The ability to use learned material in new situations

4. **Analysis** - The ability to break down material into component parts.

5. **Synthesis** - The ability to put parts together to form a new whole.

6. **Evaluation** - The ability to put parts together to judge the value of the material for a given purpose.

The Basic Process of Learning JKD:

"If you always put limits on everything you do, physical or anything else. It will spread into you work and into your life. There are no limits only plateaus. And you must not stay there. You must go beyond them."

– BRUCE LEE

When working a particular technique, make sure you learn the following:

    a. How it is done

    b. Why it is done

    c. When it is done

    d. What are the basic counters against it?

    e. What am I leaving open when I do it?

    f. How can I avoid the counter-attack?

When learning a technique, try to practice in as many ways possible to keep the student's interest.

Some Examples:

    1. With different footwork

    2. On different equipment

    3. With a partner – one on various defenses while the other attacks with it. For example, one will attack with a side kick, while the other defends. Then switch. Make sure not to always just practice an attack from a stationary stance, but also while both are moving.

That way the attacker can try to get closer to the defender before the attack, or he can attack when the defender is off balance. The attacker can also feint moving forward and then attack just as the defender starts to move. Always make every drill, as soon as you can do it as well as understand it, as alive as possible.

Follow a Realistic Training Progression:
(The JKD Triangle)

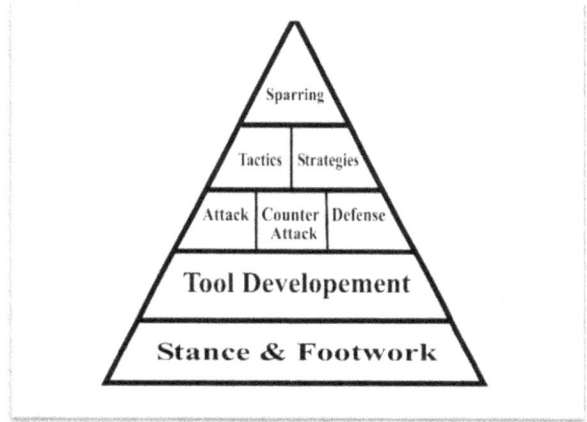

For our training we use the JKD triangle that my friend and co-author, Chris Kent, came up with. We have found it to be a great training progression.

Stance and Footwork

We start our training with stance and footwork, which are the basic foundation for our attacks and our defense.

Bruce Lee on Footwork:

1. Footwork, footwork and more footwork.

2. To go where you are safe, and he isn't.

3. Footwork can add strength and power to a punch or kick.

Always combine footwork in the techniques with the techniques you are practicing.

From footwork we start to work on developing our basic striking techniques. The art of kicking and hitting is the art of correct distance judging. along with the footwork to maintain and keep the correct distance to launch an attack. We also work on the footwork to defend against these attacks.

Tool Development

We start our tool development from are 2 basic stances, which are the on-guard and natural stance *(below)*.

 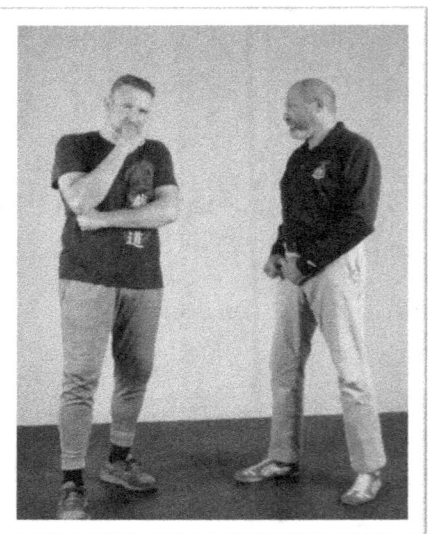

The basic method we use to train our tools is to take one and work with it first from the two basic stances. Then using different footwork. We then will take any kick or punch and work on the footwork for it. For example, in kicking there is different footwork to gain distance, to retreat from a kick or simply angling away from one. We also train footwork to quickly intercept a kick with a straight lead or stop kick. We train retreating from a kick just far enough that it just misses us. This makes it possible the counter with a punch as soon as the kicker's foot touches the floor or follow him back with a kick if he kicks and slides back to his on-guard stance. We work on moving back more than is necessary to draw a second kick, so we can move quickly forward to counter. We sometimes do that if we are surprised by the kick and retreat too far.

For example, we work all of our tools while moving forward, backwards, and angling.

The Touch the Tee Shirt Drill

This drill is done with 2 students at the fighting measure. One then attacks with a sliding side kick to the others stomach that will just missing his touching his stomach. For safety reasons the defender will have his shoulders squared so he won't get kicked in the ribs. We start at one end of the room until we reach the other end. We then reverse roles. Make sure to start slow and easy. Then slowly adding speed later. There is no reason to kick with a lot of power, but with speed and the correct distance.

We then work on different aspects of any of the tools. Once they have learned the basic technique and the footwork, we start to hone the skill.

Since our main idea of defense is to intercept our opponent's attack by seeing his preparation and then intercepting his attack, we start by getting rid of our preparation.

Work Getting Rid of Preparation.

It is natural when you are working on a technique and telegraph what you are doing slightly before you do it.

Different Common Ones

Dropping down before the attack *(below)*.

Front punch with elbow out, as you can see it easier *(below)*.

Pulling the arm back then punching *(below)*.

These are just some examples. There are many more. Watch when anybody punches or kicks and look for their preparation. The more you do this, the better you will be at seeing it. You can do this, for example, while watching a boxing match or MMA bout, either in person or on T.V.

Power Development in All Tools

Bruce Lee to Bob Bremer:

"Train so that you have sledgehammers in both hands."

"Power come from using strength quickly."
— BRUCE LEE

The Snappy Punch

The snappy punch gets its power from the speed of the speed of the punch. and the snap that occurs at the elbow when the punch is fully extended. To make sure that get the most snap, the fist only penetrates the target from I to 2 in inches. Make sure you take advantage of the "snap" to go back as quick as possible to the on- guard position or to throw a second punch like a straight rear.

The Jab vs. Straight Lead

Both the boxer's jab and the straight lead are examples of a snappy punch. The boxer's jab is mostly used to keep an opponent off balance, or as a set-up for another blow. The straight lead has the same snap at the elbow as the jab, but because it is a fully committed punch, it should only be used to intercept or as a finishing blow.

The speed jab on focus mitt *(below)*.

The Power jab on focus mitt *(below)*.

The straight lead on focus mitt *(below)*.

The Snappy Kick

A snappy kick like a hook kick gets its power from the whipping action of the leg and the snap of the knee. To get the proper whip, kick the focus glove while standing on one leg, as only way you will have power is from the whipping action of the leg.

The Scoop Kick to the Focus Glove

The Inverted Hook Kick to Focus Glove

The Snappy Hook Kick

The Whip Principle

A snappy kick like a hook kick gets its power from the whipping action of the leg and the snap of the knee. To get the proper whip, again kick the focus glove while standing on one leg.

For these 3 kicks the power comes from the whipping action of leg, by retracting the kick almost faster than the hit. Try to learn to time the snap back as soon your foot touches your opponent.

The Snappy Side Kick to the Focus Glove

The Water Hose Principle: For the side kick the power comes from your body weight and the snap of you kick at about a 3- to 4-inch penetration. Bruce Lee called it *"The Water Hose Principle,"* it's as if you were snapping the water out of a hose.

Work the kick at different distances on a kicking shield as well a focus glove. Have the student close his eyes. When the trainer has moved to a different position, have the student open his eyes and instantly kick at the right penetration and snap.

A little-known kicking principle is what Bruce Lee called the *"Rubber Band Principle."* When doing a spinning back kick drag your foot on the ground then snap it like snapping a rubber band.

The Snappy and Heavy Hitting and Kicking

Bruce Lee called them crispy and non-crispy hitting. The power from a snappy kick or punch comes the speed and snap of the tool. The advantage of snappy attack is that it is very fast in both its delivery and recovery.

The heavy hand or leg attack comes from the relaxed, heavy arm or leg hitting through the target. The advantage of a heavy strike is in its power. The disadvantage is that the recovery is slower than a snappy blow. We find it more efficient to attack with a snappy hit and follow up with a heavy finishing blow, but it can be valuable to use a heavy blow, when you are sure you can make contact, as well as when you intercept.

I learned this heavy type of hitting from my hsing-I and tai chi teachers in Taiwan. Thanks to them when I read Bruce Lee's notes, I knew exactly what he meant by crispy and uncrispy hitting and exactly how to teach them. Understand that whenever you use a heavy/uncrispy hit or kick that you are committing more time to your attack.

Work the heavy hand on the focus glove, by hitting through the target with a palm strike with a relaxed arm swing.

The Heavy Swinging Palm Hit

The Heavy Downward Palm Strike

Make sure you use the relaxed drop of your body to add weight to your attack.

The Heavy Kick

To develop power in a heavy kick like a heavy hook kick (roundhouse kick) practice the kick by trying to hit through a heavy bag, kicking shield, or Thai pad with as much penetration as possible. Once you "get it", you can then snap it back.

Reaction: The ability to react instantly in a correct manner to an attack or an opening in your opponent's defense. Reaction time is the time gap between a stimulus and the response.

We have given you some of the ways to train for this already, but it is a great idea if you can come up with your own drills for this. Be creative. Have enough different drills for the same concept or principle to make it interesting for your students.

Emotional Content = Controlled Anger

Too often students just punch and kick the focus gloves or heavy bags with no real emotions. What they should be doing is putting emotional content into every hit, so you can develop a warrior attitude. If you are attacked, you will need to learn how to let the beast loose when you need to. Bruce Lee said that it was like turning on a light bulb. You turn it on, or you turn it off. It is that fast. It helps to imagine that there's an opponent in front of you. Attack the pads, as if you are defending you loved ones. Then turn it off. Then on. As you get better at a technique when learning it, you can start adding emotional content to it. It does you no good to try add it until you can do it correctly and at full speed.

One of the drills for emotional content as well testing your conditioning was taught to me by Nicholas Hughes. The concept for the drill is simple:

1. One man holds a focus glove straight out at head height supporting it with both hands while standing straight and not moving.

2. Two students are told to imagine that this focus glove is threating someone they love and they have to destroy it.

3. When the coach yells "go," one will straight blast. or use any straight punches, by banging the hell out the focus glove, not worrying about form.

4. After about 10 seconds the other student will shove the attacker aside and start his attack. This will get faster and faster.

5. Then the other student will to the same and so on.

6. The coach will time this.

7. He will start with a 2-minute round and build up the time when they can do it for a longer period.

This drill simulates a real fight. It is chaotic with no chance to catch your breath. You can only really do this drill if you do it with emotional content.

Work on Both Snappy and Heavy Blows

Practice both heavy and snappy kick and punches and notice how much time commitment is used for each one either alone or in combination.

Work on an Airtight Defense When Attack

Even though at least 1/3 of body is open every time you attack. Be aware of where you are most vulnerable.

Open When Punching

When he leaves an opening with drawing back to hit, the defender intercepts with a rear horizontal hook *(below)*.

Stop kick as he tries a hand attack *(below)*.

Leg obstruction against a rear jab followed with a hand attack

Open When Kicking

Intercepting an attempted kick with a straight lead *(below)*.

Leg obstruction against a straight rear kick followed up with a hit to the body *(below)*.

Work on following up on your attack or quick recovery.

The attacker doesn't recover back and is hit with finger jab and an overhead rear punch as soon as his foot hits the ground. *(See photos below and on next page).*

Attack/Counter-Attack/Defense:

The third level of the pyramid progression is attack/counter attack/ defense.

On this level of the pyramid, you take a tool like a hook kick and practice all the ways you can attack with it.

Then you work on defending against it. Then you work on how to use in as a counterattack.

Finally, you need to analyze each stage for the strengths and weakness of all that you are working on. Focus on the strengths and start to eliminate the weaknesses.

Tactics and Strategy:

Your tactics and strategy will vary in any situation you might encounter and will depend on what the threat level is. Some of the these may be:

1. A friendly sparring match.

2. A sanctioned martial art match with light contact.

3. A full contact type match with rules.

4. A street fight with a way to avoid it by escaping.

5. A street fight in a crowded area.

6. A street fight with no other people around.

7. A life-or-death situation with the threat against you and/or members of your family.

Tactics are the specific actions or steps you undertake to accomplish your strategy.

Strategy is carefully developed plans or achieving a goal. or the skill in developing and undertaking such a plan or method. Below is the mental and physical process of a tactical action:

1. Perception and analysis of the situation.

2. Deciding on a solution.

3. Physical execution of the correct solution

Guidelines for Tactical Training

1. Train your powers of observation and analytical skills by:

a. Watching boxing and MMA matches. Watch to see what tactics you could use against each fighter.

b. Do the same with other fighting systems.

c. Do the same with you fellow students

d. Watching videos of street fights on YouTube to see what real street fights and attacks are really like. Watch and notice what a jumbled mess it sometimes is, and how you could train to deal it.

2. Organize your training to include tactical training.

Basic Tactics:

a. Use your head to out-think your opponent

b. Stay loose and relaxed and be ready to react to anything. that may occur. Do not be tense but be ready. Never be set, but flexible.

c. Stay calm and alert

d. Maintain a well balanced, well covered ready position.

e. As soon as your opponent comes into range HIT!

f. As soon as he starts an attack - intercept.

g. Attack on his preparation to attack, or whenever he feints or fakes an attack.

3. Work on dividing your training by these units of time:

a. Before the attack

b. During the attack

c. After the attack

You need to understand that in a real self-defense situation there is no such thing as a fair fight. You will not be the aggressor, but you need to me able to do whatever is necessary to survive, no matter how drastic or extreme. Violate the rules - cheat - bite -

attack the eyes - pick up and use improvised weapons like a pen or your keys. Do whatever it takes to be able to go home to your family. Just understand even if you do make it home safely, you may be bruised and battered.

SPARRING

"Turn your sparring into play – but play seriously."

– BRUCE LEE

Don't spar against a copy of yourself. Have your partner come at you as different fighters. You need to practice against the different types of fighters to see what works and what does not. Do not be hesitant to get rid of what does not work.

Some of the types to train against are:

1. One who blocks an attack

Feint a jab. When he parries, kick him with an inverted hook kick with a slide back to the on-guard position. *(See photos below and on next page.)*

2. *One who parries and hits*

Beat him to the punch *(See photos below and on next page)*.

3: One who blocks
Trap and back fist *(below)*.

Trap and back fist *(below)*.

Fighting a grappler is not as easy as some would have you believe. When they shoot in, they come in hard and fast. We feel that one of the worse things you can try to do to a grappler is try to attack him with either a punch or a kick. They practice shooting in so much that any attack will probably leave you wide open and ending up on the ground with him on top of you. The best strategy if he is past the fighting measure and tries to shoot in for a takedown to you is, when you see him level change, try to intercept his attack actively with a straight lead punch. Work on being able to intercept with enough power to stop the attack. When he shoots in from a close range, he will not have that much forward momentum. It is safer for you to try and intercept his attack from a close range than a longer distance.

1. Also work angling to the side to avoid the charge.

2. Don't make the mistake trying to move straight back.

3. Distance and speed of your opponent's charge will help you decide what the best course of action to take.

4. Practice – practice – then practice some more.

5. As a teacher, during any of your punching and kicking drills, add a grappling attack at any random moment and see if and how they respond.

Against a Charger

If at fighting measure. your opponent will probably not have so much momentum that you cannot stop his attack with a powerful stop hit or kick. To have enough power you need to be able to hit him with great timing and accuracy.

If he charges from a longer distance, he may have so much momentum that you can't stop him, you will need to get out of the way by angling.

4. One who shoots for a takedown

Angle out and hit (below).

Step out to push head to kick (below).

Push down of head with a knee strike to elbow attack *(below)*.

These are just a few suggestions but be prepared to be taken down.

This is because the techniques above take a lot or practice, and only have a chance of succeeding if you opponent comes at you from a distance to tackle you, which may give you the time to react. Once he is inside the fighting measure you will probably not have enough time to angle away from a good grappler's attempt to take you down from a close distance.

The best thing to do is work on defending against a good grappler is with a good grappler. Also notice what they are giving you before, during, and you are taken down.

Also work on the sprawl which you can find drills for in any good grappling book.

5. One who dances around

Sometimes you will get a guy who has seen too many movies and want to dazzle you with his fantastic footwork. It's best just keep facing him and wait for him to cross the brim of fire line, and then do a leg obstruction as a stop kick. *(See photos below and on next page).*

6. One who stop hits.

Sometimes you have an opponent that you can sense that you will be able to just thrust forward and hit him.

Sometimes you will find yourself against a JKD man, and as soon as you step forward to punch you will run into a leg obstruction *(below)*.

We teach our students that the safest way to attack is with a leg obstruction because if you do it fast enough and explode forward, he will not be able to kick, hit or retreat.

Attacking with a leg obstruction will allow you to easily follow-up with trap and hit *(below)*.

Be sure to practice against the different types of fighters when you are sparring.

Sparring Training

When you are just starting sparring, start slow and easy. Don't try to do too much when starting out. Work on both attacking with a specific tool and defending against it. Don't worry about the straight lead and intercepting when just starting out. It's a good idea to start with the boxer's jab, as it is fast and you can work on the various defenses for it, while slowly building up speed and power.

Here are just a few examples of training drills:

Basic Training:

1. A: Jab only, B: only defense.
2. Work on slipping inside and outside the jab.
3. Both only front hand with all types of hits..
4. A: Front hand only B: Only rear hand.
5. Just front kick only.
6. Only front hand and foot.
7. Both all hands.
8. Both all feet.
9. All tools.
10. Add shoot at any time.
11. Two against two.
12. Two against three.
13. Two on for four. The two try to break through the four as if escaping an alley
14. Create your own

If you are an instructor, make sure your students keep switching partners. That way they get used to working with different people. People who:

1. Are taller or shorter so you need to adjust to a different fighting measure.

2. Have a different rhythm than you have.

3. Are faster or slower than you.

4. Specialize in different tools than you like and attack with different kicks or hand attacks.

5. Use distance, or attacks by entering into your range.

These are just a few examples. Add you own.

Train Realistically, But Safely.

When I was studying to become a high school teacher, I read an article by Neil Postman on education. He said that the purpose of education was to give the student a built in BS detector. The main purpose of Jeet Kune Do is to give you that detector. I think that if you follow the principles and analyze what you are doing, you are off to a good start. Another thing you can do is test what you are learning against someone who is trying to actively trying to stop what you are doing. A lot of techniques may work against someone who is no good, or from your same school. It is good if you have friends from different martial arts you can work with. How do you know if you can stop a takedown from a good grappler without testing it? The problem is if he charges in like a ton of bricks, how can you stop him with an intercepting punch of kick without really hurting him? I don't really have great answer for that except start slow and easy. Then you can build up speed and power slowly. If you are taken down then, work on how to get back to your feet as quickly as you can. Just try and test what you do in as many alive drills as you can against your attacks as well as defenses as possible and as safe as possible.

Shadow Boxing

One of the best ways for a teacher to anglicize his student's progress and to decide what to work on is by having the entire class do a few rounds of shadow boxing.

Some things to look for:

1. Are they covering when they attack.

2. Are they visualizing someone attacking them and reacting efficiently.

3. Is their footwork fluid and balanced.

4. Are they moving with a steady or broken rhythm.

5. What is his relationship to the other moving students.

The instructor can then tailor his teaching to what he is seeing. We always have the students shadow box right after they have warmed up.

The Wall Survival Drill

We learned the wall survival drill from Bert Poe in my garage. Bert had been a boxer in the Marines. It has become our go-to exercise before we start hard sparring. It simulates being cornered or up against a wall, while been hit with a flurry of punches. It will help teach the student how to survive in the ring if cornered, injured or against the rope. It's Ali's "rope a dope."

The idea is to cover for a certain amount of time until the trainer says to either get away from the wall or clinch. The person being hit is in complete charge of the exercise. He tells the puncher to hit either softer or harder. He tells him to punch faster or slower.

The wall drill in action *(photos below and on following pages):*

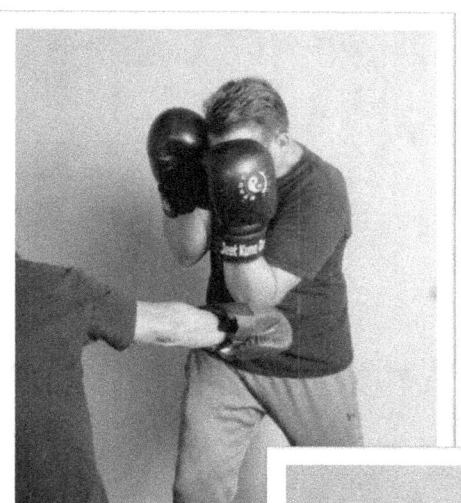

ATTRIBUTES

Timing

Reaction Time is the time taken between a movement -- the "stimulus" -- and a student's response to that movement. Movement time is the time taken to execute a motion.

Timing is also the ability to seize an opportunity when you see it.

The McCann Drill

This drill was shown to us by one of our instructors, Jim McCann. Our group has been lucky enough to attract people who join our group who are very good in some other martial art or have been a student of another JKD instructor. At our seminars we take advantage of this by having our instructors share some what they have learned on their own or from other instructors.

To do this drill have the trainer with a focus glove and the student farther away or right at the fighting measure. He then:

1. Keeping the mitt steady he steps forward with his front foot, while the student intercepts. *(See photos on next page.)*

2. Sometimes the trainer will step forward very deep forcing the student to step back and punch *(below)*.

3. Sometimes when the trainer steps forward you can intercept his attack by moving forward *(below)*.

4. Sometimes you will intercept later *(below)*.

5. Sometimes the trainer will take a quick, deep step forward with his rear leg forcing the student to step back and punch *(below)*.

6. Sometimes you can intercept him as he steps forward (*below*).

> *"A man is always in a learning process. Whereas "style is a concluding, established something. You cannot do that as you grow every day, you must not be limited to one approach."*
>
> – BRUCE LEE

7. Sometimes he will step forward so fast that you need to angle outside to avoid the glove *(below)*.

Do the drill by varying the speed, distance, and the timing to make the drill as alive as possible. Also, occasionally level drop and come in with the glove waist high simulating a grappler's shooting in. The student will then need to level change and intercept with a punch. This drill is designed to work on your distance and timing while intercepting. You can also come up the drills for kicking with various equipment for the same reason.

Know That the Ring and Street Are Different.

Most students of martial arts know that fighting in the ring and the street are different. They mention that in the ring there is a referee, rounds with a time limit, and rules. While in the street, there is none of that. But one of the main reasons it is different is something few have thought about, and that is is prior knowledge. When you fight in the ring, for the most part, you will know who your opponent will be. There's probably some film of his prior fights for you to look at. If not, you will have some idea of his training and what it focuses on. Is he mainly a striker or a grappler? You will almost always have some idea about your opponent.

None of this will happen in a street encounter. You will probably only find out after you are attacked. This is why focusing on intercepting with power is the best method for street survival. If you have control of the distance between the two of you, should be able to intercept his attack. I just hope you have developed enough power to make it work.

Engage in Environmental Training.

Try to get out of the gym or school and train in different environments.

Some Examples:

1. On a hillside
2. On gravel
3. On sand
4. On a slippery surface
5. Create your own

Daily Minimize, Not Daily Increase.

A sculptor doesn't keep adding clay to his subject. Actually, he keeps chiseling away at the non-essentials until the truth is revealed without obstructions. The more complicated and restricted the method, the less the opportunity for the expression of one's original sense of freedom. Though they play an important role in the early stage of training.

The point of the hot stove story shows the danger of relying on too many responses to a single stimulus. Why would you need 15 different responses to a simple boxing jab? Bruce Lee called such training "organized despair".

"Being wise does not mean to 'add' more. Being wise means to be able to get off sophistication and be simply simple."

– BRUCE LEE

Hicks Law: The time it takes to make a decision increases with the number and complexity of choices.

Coordination, Agility and Balance.

To be able to be efficient in any martial art you need to have the coordination, agility, and balance to make any technique work. Some of us are born with great agility, coordination and balance, while some are not. Everybody needs to work on this no matter good they are. Even if you are rather awkward, just the martial art practice alone will improve your coordination. I was lucky that I spent every afternoon and most of the day on Saturday at our local YMCA from 1st grade until I graduated from high school. Our Redlands YMCA was known for the circus they put on every year. I started doing basic tumbling in grades 1 to 4. Then I had an act where I walked on top of a large wooden ball up a ramp to end up on top of a platform. Around 8 grade I joined a trampoline act with 1 adult and a college student. I did that act until I graduated from high school. Even if I was in a play, practicing football, or running track, I still went to circus practice at night. All this really gave me the ability to know at all times just where my body was in space. The circus really helped me. Try to stay as active as possible play sports with your friends. You can even take a dance class or tai chi.

Coordination Practice Examples:

a. Take sequence like the boxer's jab, cross and hook and reverse them hook, cross and jab.

b. Practice footwork on different surfaces where you normally train like sand, gravel, on a hill or a slick surface.

c. Do an entire training session on the opposite lead you are used to being in.

Agility Practice Examples:

a. In your stance, move quickly forward, backwards, sideways and at an angle. Vary your distance and speed.

b. Run forward with high knees.

c. Lateral Running, Side-to-Side

d. Your own example

Balance:

a. Stand on one foot and hop and punch a focus glove, while the coach moves forward and back. After thirty seconds switch feet.

b. Practice all kicks on a focus glove while standing on one leg.

c. Add balance training to your everyday life. For example, always put your shoe while standing on one leg.

d. Your own example.

Speed = Train Different Types of Speed.

Come up with different drills using focus gloves and other equipment, as well as drills with a partner for all of the different types of speed.

Perceptual Speed: Quickness of eye -- so you when you see an attack coming toward you can judge the distance, and its trajectory so you can devise the proper counterattack. It also means that you can see any opening in his defense as it occurs.

Mental Speed: Mental speed is the ability to take advantage of what the mind sees. The eye will see an opening, and the mind reacts to it, and decides what course of action to take

Initiation Speed: This means that to take advantage of mental speed you need to what Bruce Lee called economical starting. This mean that you are able to fire a punch or kick as quickly as possible.

Performance Speed: This is simply how fast a punch travels from point A to point B.

Recovery Speed: This is simply how fast you can recover back to an on-guard position, or to follow up with another attack.

Alteration Speed: This is how long it takes you to change from one attack to another one, if a different line opens up. In other words, you start and attack, and as you do you see another opening appear and switch your attack to that line.

Sensitivity Speed: This is the ability to be able when you have any contact with your opponent and feel any opening as they occur and then be able to react to it.

To be fast, you must be able to use all of the above speeds.

Accuracy and Precision

Precision can be defined as accuracy in a particular movement or projection of force. To be able to do maximum damage to your opponent, you need to deliver your attack to either a stationary or moving target to the precise area to do the most damage.

First work on accuracy then on speed and power.

One of the best methods to develop accuracy is training with focus gloves.

1. Paint a white dot on the focus glove right where the center of your palm, as it will probably not be in the exact center of your focus glove but probably a little lower.

2. Hit the focus glove when the trainer moves it as you punch and kick it while the glove is still moving.

3. Practice hitting and kicking the top and bottom bag.

4. Hang a tennis ball and practice kicking it at different heights.

5. Your own example.

Awareness

If you train long enough you may develop an unconscious awareness where you can sometimes just react without thought. If you train something long enough and correctly you may be able to simply just react without thought. It will happen that someday when someone throws a punch, and you intercept him, you don't hit. It just happens.

> *"As I get older my speed may decrease,
> but my awareness will increase."*
>
> – BRUCE LEE

Vision Awareness = *Learning to see something quickly and to react to it. To do that you need fast eyes and speedy hands.*

Some Drills for Vision Awareness

Trainer has two gloves on his chest and then flashes it for a different punch or a kick.

Straight lead punch
(Photo at right.)

Front Hook Punch *(top)* or Back Fist *(middle photo)*; *Side Kick (bottom photo)*.

Hook Kick
(top photo);

Inverted Hook Kick
(bottom photo).

Then work different combinations:

Trainer one hand on chin and one at waist.

    a. Raise finger at chin student will punch

    b. Raise finger at waist student will kick

Environmental Awareness

Location

Things to Look for:

1. If you are in a building, where are the exits and what is around you?

2. Are there any things you can use at a weapon?

3. Is it an isolated area? Are you alone, or are there other people?

4. Try and train in different environments like a beach, a crowded room, or an enclosed space

5. What else can you come up with?

Opponent

To be aware at all times against an opponent or possible opponent's action, impending action or reaction. The more aware you are the better you are prepared to deal with that person.

At the Smokey Mountain Summer Camp, I would sit with Bert Poe, and we would watch people walk by. Bert would then tell me how he would fight. He would tell me if he would be a brawler and charged straight in, or if he would be more of a defensive fighter. He gave even more information about each person. Later when I saw them spar, Bert was correct about each and every one just by seeing how they walked.

Situational Awareness

Anytime you are in a situation that can lead to violence you need to:

1. Figure the threat level

2. Can you just get out of there?

3. If you can't leave, your tactics and strategy will depend on how serious the threat level is, and who is with you, or if you are alone

4. Then act accordingly.

Avoid Steady Rhythm Training.

When a lot of our students train, they seem to do it at a steady rhythm. I also see this in any school I visit, or seminar I have taught at, or even just watched. Every drill or series of techniques from hitting the focus gloves to attacking or defensive training seems to end up in a steady rhythm. This is a bad habit because is easy and natural for you and your training partner to fall into a steady rhythm and is much easier to train with a steady rhythm. It is much harder to "fit in" to a broken rhythm. Make sure to look for this when you either train or watch people train. Try to observe and be aware of the rhythm of the fighters in martial art and boxing matches as well as any of the fighters' preparation to their attacks.

THE HAMMER PRINCIPLE

The Hammer Principle is one of the best drills that you can do, as it helps make both your attacks and defense better and more efficient. The reason most students don't get it, is they don't put the time in practicing it.

To train the hammer principle you need a partner.

To practice the hammer principle, one will try and touch the other on the forehead with a finger jab or their palm, while the other one tries to parry it. You and you partner need to stand far enough apart so that the attacker has to step forward to touch you. You can't be so far apart that it is too hard to score a hit, or stand too close to make it too easy. Vary the distance to adjust for your getting better. If you can score most of your hits, start from a longer distance. Aim for about a 50/50 success rate. That way both the attacker and the defender will improve.

Both at fighting measure with A's hand outstretched with a finger jab about 6 inches from B's forehead *(below)*.

The one being attacked hands should not be so far apart so that it is too hard to parry, or to be so close that it is too easy to parry. Try to make it so the parries and hits are about equal.

The key to the drill is for the one being attacked will act as a trainer, by pointing out when he parries the attack what he saw that enabled him to parry it. He looks for and tries to rid the attacker of all his preparation as he attacks. What will happen is that both of the will get better and better, as the attacker will become more efficient, as will the defender. After a long time once you have gotten rid of all of the attacker's preparation, you may be able to intercept on his intention to attack. To do this, you don't hit. It hits.

Dropping the Hammer

You drop the arm from the elbow only. Nothing else moves. It is as if you are hammering a nail. You need to make sure that your hand is even with your partner's nose. If it is too high, it will be too easy to see it. If it is too low, there is no way to drop your arm *(photos below)*.

This shows that you have gained a closer distance between your hand and his forehead. The trick is to drop the hammer at the same time as you thrust your body forward to attack. This is very hard to do fast and with no preparation. Don't give up and you will get it. You will be able to hit without preparation but be able to see any opponent's preparation *(below)*.

Dropping the hammer -- front view *(below)*.

The entire attack sequence:

BRUCE LEE'S DRAGON STORY

If you have read this book, you should be able to understand the meaning of this story -- a fable as told to Bob Bremer by Bruce Lee.

According to Bob Bremer, Bruce Lee was fond of telling stories as way to explain a martial art principle. Bob told the Wednesday Night Group that most of the stories included an old Chinese man of some sort. One of the stories that Bruce told Bob was the story about a woodcutter and a dragon. Bob told us that after Bruce told the story he would just smile and walk away and never mention the story again. He also would never bother to explain the meaning of the story leaving it up to the listener to figure it out. I hope you can understand the meaning. One person having heard Bob tell the story published a version of it in a European martial art magazine. He then tried to explain the meaning of the story, but got the point of it completely wrong. I hope you do better.

Here's the story:

The Woodcutter and the Dragon

Once upon a time, there was an old Chinese woodcutter. He was very poor. Every day, he went out into the forest hoping to chop enough wood to sell in the town to make enough money to buy rice to feed his family. One day when he was deep in the forest cutting down a tree with his trusty axe, he heard a giant roar from behind on the other side of a clearing. He heard the roar again and saw that the trees were shaking as if there was a huge windstorm. Since the wind was calm where he was, he couldn't figure out what was happening on the other side of the clearing.

He soon found out because a huge dragon suddenly appeared. The woodcutter immediately thought to himself, "If I could kill this dragon, I could sell it for so much money that I could feed my family for the rest of my life and never have to cut wood again". The woodcutter then grabbed his axe and took a step toward the dragon.

The dragon then raised a claw with huge talons on it and said, "Hold it right there you SOB. I know what you want to do. You want to kill me with that axe so you can sell my body for a lot of money. Well, I'm telling you that if you take one more step, I'll blow my fiery breath on you and burn you to a cinder."

The woodcutter figured it was no use to try and kill the dragon, so he turned his back on him and went back to chopping the tree down. The second time he went to chop the tree the axe slipped out of his hand and hit the dragon right between the eyes killing him.

J. Krishnamurti:
The Joke About the Devil

You may remember the story of how the Devil and a friend of his were walking down the street, when they saw ahead of them a man stoop down and pick something from the ground, look at it, and put it away in his pocket.

The friend said to the Devil, "What did that man pick up?"

"He picked up a piece of Truth," said the Devil.

"That is a very bad business for you then," said his friend.

"Oh, not at all," the Devil replied. "I am going to let him organize it."

Always remember that the Truth is always outside of all fixed patterns.

-- J. Krishnamurti

CONCLUSION

What it all means:

> *"There is no one way; there is only one way that works in a given moment of time."*
>
> – BRUCE LEE

Whether you are a Jeet Kune Do student or teacher when you teach a technique, make sure to explain what the principle is in what you are teaching, and why you are teaching it.

If you are from another martial art discipline, figure out how can you use the principles in the book for your own training.

It all boils down to this:

Bruce Lee said that Jeet Kune Do is "Western sword fighting without the sword"

To stress one more time as it bears repeating, JKD is:

1. Keeping a safe distance, so that to attack you with anything but a projectile weapon, your opponent must step toward you.

2. This gives you the time to react to stop the attack.

3. You need to see the attack that is coming and react to stop it.

4. You need to have enough power to end the fight as fast as possible.

5. Learn how to stay on your feet.

6. If taken to the ground, learn how to get back on your feet as soon as possible.

That may sound easy but is takes a long time to learn how to really do it.

The Purpose of Jeet Kune Do:

To give you a built-in bullshit detector. I hope this book can start you on that path.

Being a Teacher:

> "A teacher is never a giver of truth;
> he is a guide, a pointer to the truth that each student
> must find for himself"
>
> – BRUCE LEE

> "Life itself is your teacher, and you are in a
> state of constant learning."
>
> – BRUCE LEE

Frequently Asked Questions:

How long will it take me to become a JKD instructor?
The same time as it would take you to be a good basketball player and then a coach.

Are there any JKD masters?
There are no JKD masters. because you are always in a process of learning. The quest to get better never goes away.

As Bruce Lee said:

> *"Once you are a master, the lid on your coffin is starting to close.*

THE END

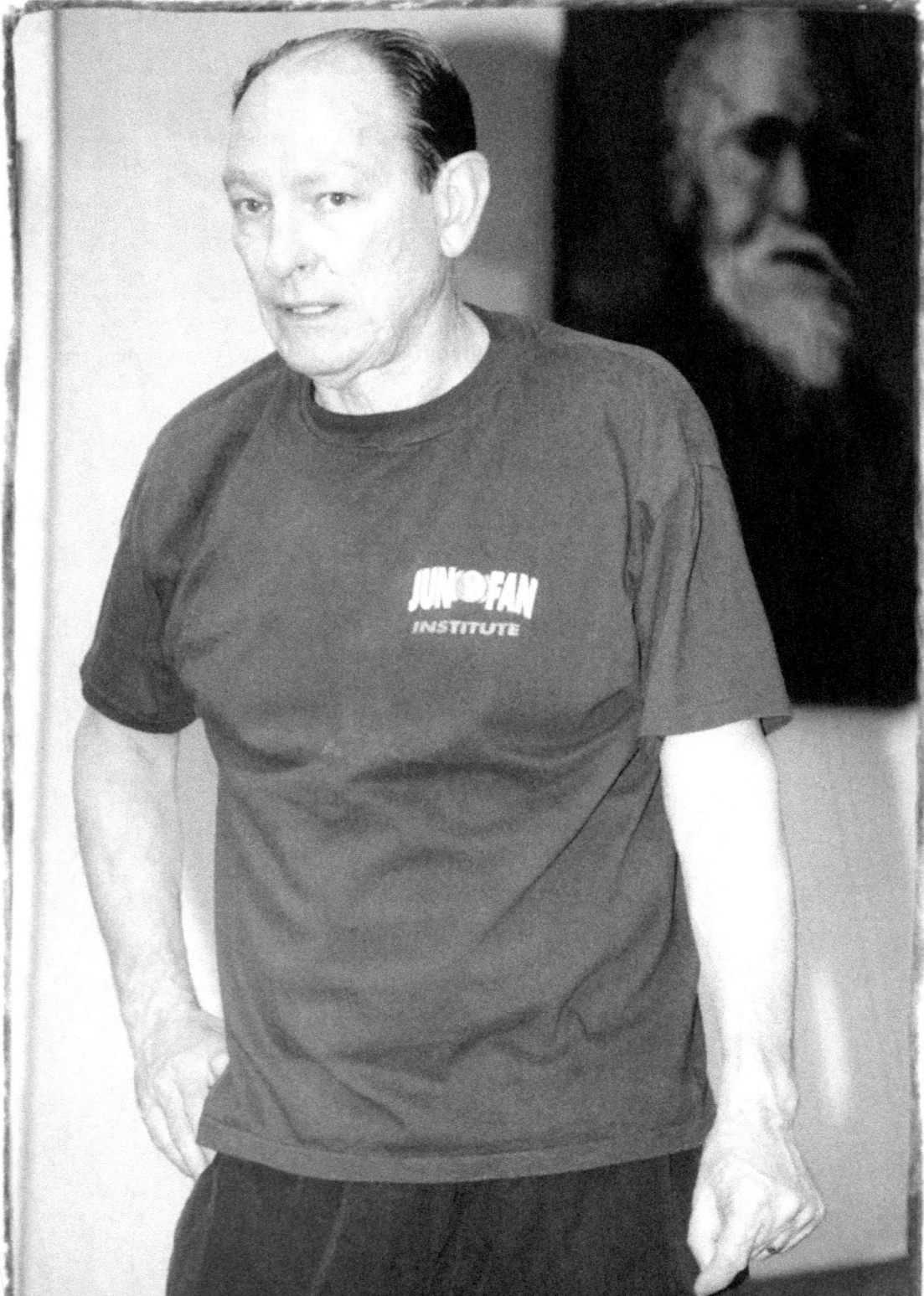

One-on-One with TIM TACKETT

When did you begin your martial arts training?

"During my stay in Taiwan from early 1962 to the end of 1964 as a member of the Air Force, I studied *Hsing-I*, which is an internal system but also very effective for fighting. I also had training in other arts such as tai chi, northern Shaolin, southern Shaolin and White Crane Gung-fu."

How did you get started in Jeet Kune Do?

"In the 1960s I was teaching kung fu to help me get through college. I finally received my MFA in acting and directing and started teaching high school drama in 1970. Around 1971 I felt the need to do something different, or at the very least add on to my tai chi knowledge. I decided to go to Los Angeles to a tai chi school with my first Chinese martial art student, Bob Chapman. When we went there the instructor asked me about my background, and I told him what I had learned in Taiwan. He asked me to show him the tai chi that my teacher taught me. After I showed him the tai chi form, for he said that his accepted both of us as students. When we were leaving and got outside of his school, his assistant followed us outside. He came up to us and said that we were not going to learn anything from this instructor, as my prior training was a threat to him. I was really shocked. He asked if we knew about and Jeet Kune Do and Bruce Lee. I told him that Bob and I had both seen him at Ed Parker's 1967 Tournament, and I saw him when he was a guest at a karate tournament and said "Hello" to him. I had seen him demonstrate at Parker's tournament and was impressed with his skill. I had also read some Black Belt Magazine articles about him and his art. I was interested in learning JKD, but was too busy with school and teaching kung fu for most nights and on Saturdays, I did not have the time to drive the 70 miles to his school. When I said "Hello" to he him, Bruce nodded to me. I almost asked him about joining his school but quickly decided that since I did not have the time, it was pointless and just moved on. By the time I finished my college work he had closed his L.A. Chinatown School.

When Dan Lee asked me if I was interested in JKD and we answered "yes", he said that his number one assistant, Dan Inosanto, was teaching in his backyard because Bruce Lee had closed down his Chinatown school. The person telling me this was Dan Lee. I don't know the reason why he did that because it was a very private group. He gave me Sifu Dan's private phone number. I knew Dan pretty well having met him met him at Parker's school shortly after getting out of the US Air Force late in 1964. Ed Parker asked me s to show him what I had learned in Taiwan. I did and after the class ended Dan Inosanto and Steve Golden asked me to go to dinner with them. I saw Dan a lot at various karate type tournaments, so I went ahead and called Dan Inosanto. He invited me to come to his backyard school and that I could bring Bob Chapman, and that's how I began training in Jeet Kune Do with my friend Bob Chapman."

Who was training in that group?

"Some of the Bruce Lee students in Chinatown like Dan Lee, Bob Bremer, Richard Bustillo, Jerry Poteet, Pete Jacobs and Tony Luna were in the class. A few years later Sifu Inosanto opened another class with Ted LucayLucay, Jeff Amada and Chris Kent. Bob and I started on a Thursday night in 1972. The classes were Tuesday and Thursday night from 7:00 to 9:00 for Jeet Kune Do and 9:00 to 10:00 if you wanted to stay to learn Escrima. Chapman would pick me up at five o'clock from where

I was teaching high school and would drive for 90 minutes to Dan's house. We would stop and eat on the way home. I would not get home until around one o'clock in the morning. Then get up at six and drive 40 minutes to teach high school drama.

That first night, Dan had told us to bring 16-ounce boxing gloves. I ended standing there with 16-ounce gloves and sparing with these guys with 12- and 14-ounce gloves. The first night I had to spar with Bob Bremer and Danny Lee. Sparing with them was a real eye opener. I quickly realized that while I knew a lot more techniques than they did, I was no match for them when to applying what I had learned. When we first got to class, Sifu Inosanto handed us some sheets of paper with some of Bruce Lee's philosophy. One of the saying was that it is not what you know that is important. It's what you can apply in combat that is counts. Instead of being discouraged, Chapman and I really were inspired to learn as much as we can. For us, JKD was love at first sight."

What did the training focus on?

"The training was in Jeet Kune Do – it was not called *Jun Fan Gung Fu,* or "JKD Concepts." My first certificate reads, "Jeet Kune Do." The classes were two hours every Tuesday and Thursday, and we only practiced Escrima after class for about an hour. Technique wise, we drilled JKD basics such as the straight lead punch, and footwork. We used different equipment like focus gloves, kicking shields, and heavy bags. We worked on trying to intercept the opponent's action from the very beginning, which is the essential element of Jeet Kune Do. Which means: *The Way Of The Intercepting Fist.*"

What was Jeet Kune Do in 1971?

"It was a system that had been developed a few years ago with just a bunch of students practicing. No seminars, no videotapes, no hundreds of instructors around the world – just Dan Inosanto in Los Angeles, Taky Kimura's group which was mostly modified

Wing Chun, the Oakland guys, Plus Larry Hartsell had a small group in North Carolina. That was it. Very few people in martial arts knew what is or much about it. Very people knew about the art. We felt privileged to be a part of this exclusive art. We were not encouraged to teach any of it outside of class."

Are the terms "Jun Fan gung fu" and "Jeet Kune Do" two different things?

"The name of the school was The Jun Fan Gung Fu Institute, but the art of JKD was never named "Jun Fan Gung Fu" until Bruce Lee passed away. Inosanto promised Bruce Lee to never commercialize the art. When the seminars started around 1975, people who attended wanted to receive some kind of certificate of attendance. So the hosts were told to make the certificates read "Jun Fan Gung Fu. Later on, Inosanto opened the old Kali

Academy in Torrance, California. He was into the Filipino arts and he didn't want to push Jeet Kune Do too openly, so he began to call it Jun Fan gung fu. We just called it "Jeet Kune Do" like we did in the backyard classes, because that's what it was – JKD. "Jun Fan" was the term Bruce used to describe his modified version of Wing Chun that included a few things from other Chinese systems. You can say that Jun Fan was the forerunner of Jeet Kune Do. Actually, Jun Fan Gung Fu really means Bruce Lee's art, which was Jeet Kune Do. So, in a way they are both really JKD."

But what about the Jun Fan Gung Fu Institute in Chinatown?

"It was the place where people practiced the gung-fu system developed by Jun Fan (Bruce Lee)–but Bruce's system was called "Jeet Kune Do." JKD is really mainly a mixture of three different elements– Western fencing, Western boxing and Wing

Chun, plus a few techniques from a few other arts. On the other hand, if you look at his philosophical notes, Bruce was greatly influenced by Taoism, Zen, and Jiddu Krishnamurti but, interestingly enough, he was heavily influenced by Western philosophy also—which gave him pragmatism and the scientific method at the same time. I think this particular approach helped him to synthesize philosophy with physical combat."

 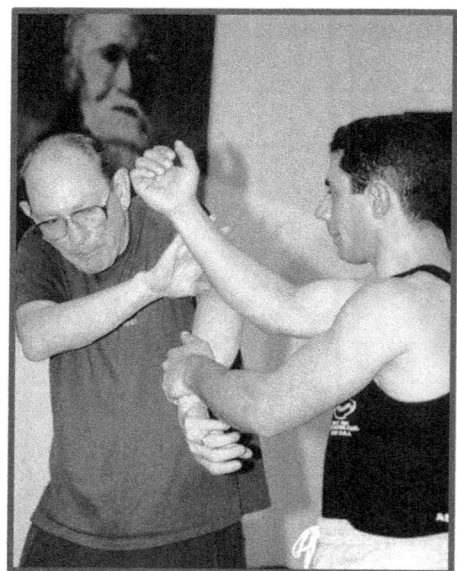

Why do some people call it "Jun Fan gung fu" instead of "Jeet Kune Do?"

"Because the name *Jeet Kune Do* was directly related to Bruce Lee and neither one of us wanted to capitalize on Bruce's name to promote ourselves or the art. None of us really wanted to teach full time or advertise. In 1974, Sifu Inosanto gave me permission to teach a few people in my garage. So, I started with a few guys on Wed night in my garage. Around that time Dan Inosanto was being constantly asked to teach Jeet Kune Do, but he was not really happy with that idea. Inosanto wanted the JKD to continue but he didn't want to teach JKD openly because he had made a promise to Bruce not to do so. So, he decided that he would just call it "Jun Fan martial arts." When the summer

seminars started Sifu Dan asked Larry Hartsell and me to teach. I think the major reason I was asked is that I, as a schoolteacher, I had summers off and was available. The more senior guys had full time regular jobs and couldn't get off work as most the seminars lasted for 4 to 6 weeks."

What about "JKD Concepts?"

"This is a way of describing an attitude toward the martial arts, but unfortunately its use has caused many misunderstandings. You can use some of the Jeet Kune Do principles and concepts to analyze and improve other arts that you practice or teach, but that doesn't mean those arts are JKD. The name became an umbrella term to practice four or five different styles and relate them to Jeet Kune Do for commercial purposes. There's nothing wrong with using a training method from savate or Thai boxing to improve certain physical attributes very important in Jeet Kune Do, but it doesn't make savate or Thai boxing "Jeet Kune Do."

You can "intercept" in Thai boxing, savate, or kali, but none of these arts is Jeet Kune Do. Some of these arts use things that break some of the basic principles and fundamental techniques of JKD. For example, leaving the groin open on entries, not trapping effectively, not having an airtight defense. I don't practice jiu-jitsu and call it JKD. It is not fair to the jiu-jitsu people to take their stuff and call it something else—that's not an honorable thing to do. You may train in jiu-jitsu, Thai boxing and pull out a few things because of the JKD principles—but they are still jiu-jitsu and Thai boxing, not JKD. Many instructors wrongly present a mishmash of martial arts techniques and call it "Jeet Kune Do."

Is JKD a style?

"Bruce never wanted JKD to be a style. Thirty years ago the term "style" was something very closed and had a negative connotation to Bruce. In the 1960s and 70s, everyone stuck to one style like Shotokan karate and didn't train outside of their particular style. Bruce Lee felt that that was too confining. Today the styles are much more open than before and usually adapted a lot of things from other arts. Bruce Lee never wanted JKD to be a closed system, but he had a JKD structure, a JKD base, and certain JKD techniques.

JKD is not a do-whatever-you-want approach. You can't just put a little bit of this and a little bit of that together and magically end up with JKD. When he opened the Kali Academy, he brought to two backyard classes as a private group and continued learning JKD. He then started teaching Jun Fan that he had divided into 4 phases. Once a student learned all 4 phases, he would be voted into the closed door JKD group."

But haven't you added a few things to the fundamental JKD structure?

"Yes, but we don't call it "Jeet Kune Do." We use JKD as a base or a foundation – everything else has to fit onto that foundation. There are some good things that we use from other martial arts like Thai boxing, jiu-jitsu, or shoot wrestling, but we don't call them JKD. We call them Thai boxing, jiu-jitsu or shoot wrestling. I think it is important to give credit where credit is due. I think we added some very good things that I'm sure Bruce would have liked. JKD didn't end with Bruce Lee in Los Angeles, but JKD is not adding other disciplines to the art either. The key is having an understanding of how to stick to the principles.

You see, if you don't really understand JKD principles and techniques, you can't add anything want and call it JKD. Adding for the sake of adding is not a JKD attitude because you may be adding the things that go against the basic principles of JKD because you lack deep understanding of a basic JKD technique. For instance, according to Bruce's writings, "JKD has a tight structure in defense in attack." So why are some people adding to the JKD core entry techniques with the groin wide open, or passive moves that rely on the student blocking and then hitting against a punch instead of using the leg obstruction or a stop hit? The answer is because they lack JKD understanding. You don't add something you don't need or something that goes against the basic principles of the art. You need the roots, period.

Without roots, people get confused and end up without a structure to grow from. No criteria and no guidelines equal no learning. You can't learn everything at the same time. You need a strong core of something to develop from. It's like having a bunch of branches with no trunk. You need the roots, and you need the trunk — that's what Jeet Kune Do is for us. But it is true that JKD is a very individual thing, and everybody is a bit different. There is a level in JKD where you can't teach the student anymore. This is because JKD's highest level is about personal expression in combat. How are you going to teach somebody to express himself? You can help him, and you can teach him how to get it, but his personal expression will come from him, not from you.

The problem is that many people think that they are capable of expressing themselves when they really don't understand what Jeet Kune Do is all about. You can't learn your "self-expression" through Jeet Kune Do without having a teacher who knows how to guide you from A to Z. You need the core understanding of how the philosophy works and how it affects the physical art. I really believe that JKD provides a way for everybody to create their own path, and not to just blindly follow another's."

How good was Bruce Lee?

"Ed Parker said to another karate legend that Bruce was "walking death." Enough said. He was living proof of the idea of "daily decrease." This means that you get a few things down so well that you don't really need anything else. From what I understand, by the time of his death, Bruce didn't need to use anything other than a finger jab. That's what a JKD man looks for; to get something so everybody should learn it, but everybody

has his or her personal preferences. Personally, I don't want to focus on grappling, I want to focus on defending against grappling. But in order to do that, I need to understand grappling. So, you need to learn how to grapple, but you don't have to be fixated on grappling if you can train to avoid it. The art of JKD provides the freedom to not be bound by any technique—including the fundamentals if necessary—and to evolve and grow in your own process of existence. Since I am an educator by profession, I've always believed that the purpose of teaching is to give people a "BS Detector," so they can look at something and see by themselves if it is good or not. They need to learn to ask themselves any time they are learning a new technique when I am attacking an opponent with this technique what am I leaving open to a counter-attack? You need to also ask yourself, 'What is the best way to counter this attack?' This is an important part of the learning process in JKD. Unfortunately. this is seldom done in some JKD schools."

How are you perpetuating Jeet Kune Do?

"I'm teaching my group in Redlands, California. Bob Bremer used to help me teach, and he was very helpful by opening our eyes to how to see JKD in the reality of combat. Jeremy Lynch and Dennis Blue do most of the teaching now that I am retired."

Some people say that because of Bruce Lee's sudden death, the art of Jeet Kune Do is incomplete.

"I don't think so. I'm sure Bruce would have evolved and added some good things. Maybe grappling is the only aspect that wasn't stressed much then. If JKD had any one thing that it was not strong at, it would be the grappling. But these days, a lot of great grapplers are JKD people. Grappling is good and was teaching to my students and give his personal opinion about it. Because of Bob's JKD knowledge, I quickly found out that roughly 90 percent of all the things I was teaching years ago were inefficient. I had partially lost that "critical eye" that is JKD. I was exploring, researching, and trying many arts without using JKD as a filter to look at them. Combat is either efficient or inefficient and, in terms of efficiency Bob Bremer was at the top of the class."

Why is it sometimes said that JKD is an art that cannot be taught?

"The JKD core can be taught. but the other side of the coin is that because JKD's highest level is self-expression, no teacher can teach you at a "postgraduate" level. In a sense, at that point, Jeet Kune Do cannot be taught. I remember Dan Inosanto telling us that going to your teacher and learning a technique is like going to a man every day for a fish. You become dependent on the man who gives you the fish. So, the real challenge of a JKD teacher is to teach the student to fish for himself and to become an independent thinker. That's what I like to do with my students."

JKD is based on three essential principles: directness, simplicity and a non-classical approach according to Bruce Lee's personal notes. Would you elaborate a little bit on these conceptual elements of the art of Jeet Kune Do?

"Directness simply means to go from point A to point B with the most efficient way possible. For example, while a straight finger jab to the eyes may be the fastest and most direct, don't be bound by it. Sometimes a curved line may be more efficient when taking what your opponent is offering you by leaving an opening.

Simplicity means just what the word means. When someone throws a ball to you, you simply catch it. You don't jump into a stance. Bruce Lee believed that there were too many complex moves in classical Chinese martial arts. He believed one should "strip the unessential".

You need to learn have a non-classical approach and not be bound by any classical style. This will allow the student to find his own way by using some basic principles of combat. Remember a principle is not a particular technique, but rather a guide. For example, to intercept your opponent's attack is a principle, but doesn't tell you exactly what technique to use."

How a martial artist from other style can use and apply these essential concepts to their arts?

"Take any of the principles in the book and analyze them in the things that you do. For example, using the time commitment theory on any of the techniques you are learning to see if you can find a way to lessen the time it takes to do something. It's all about self-discovery."

What happens if the practitioner of this "given style" (karate, kenpo, jiu jitsu, etc.) by following these principles needs to start changing things in their "style," and their style starts to "look" different from the original method that he/she learned from their instructor?

"This will depend on what the martial artist wants to do with what he has learned. Years ago, a non-contact Korean karate champion wanted to enter the new full contact kickboxing contests. He found that his footwork and karate type punches did not work against the kickboxers he started working with. He contacted me and I helped him learn JKD footwork and boxing hands. He needed no help on his kicking. He later became a kickboxing champion as well as holding some boxing championships.

In truth, if you are really trying to understand the principles, then what you are doing will no longer look exactly what you learned from your instructor. Bruce Lee said that too many classical martial arts try to "fit everyone into the same sized jacket." This is why Bruce Lee taught different things to private students. While both Bob Bremer and Ted Wong both taught what they learned Bruce, it looked different. Ted being smaller worked more on footwork for attacking and defense, Bob being bigger would crash in as he intercepted the attack. When I was training in Sifu Dan Inosanto's backyard class, he made sure that we did not become a clone of our teacher. We found our own way to "express ourselves". We try to do this in our own teaching, by showing different ways to illustrate a particular principle."

Please give us some ideas of how a Tae Kwon Do or Karate practitioner can use the JKD principles?

"Just take a principle and analyze how it works in the techniques they are working on. If they think that the principle has value but does not work well with what they are doing, they have to either change the technique or ignore the principle."

What about a Wing Chun man, being the hand movements closer to the art of JKD?

"When we started the Bruce Lee Foundation Seminars, we included instructors from all three eras of JKD. We had lessons from instructors from the Seattle School, the Oakland school and the Los Angeles Chinatown School. The Seattle school stressed a modified version of Wing Chun. The Oakland school added boxing hands, footwork, and training methods from boxing, while the L.A. school was influenced by Western fencing. The Seattle

School's stance, footwork and main method of defense was very different. It was easier to do what the instructors from Oakland were teaching than what the Seattle guys were doing. For example, Wing Chun focuses on blocking and hitting at the same time. While that was taught in the L.A. school, the focus was more on the fencing principle intercepting before you need to block. A lot of the trapping was the same, but not much else. While some of the L.A. guys did the Wing Chun blast, some of us do more of what we call JKD blast.

The structure was so different that most of us kept only 1/3 of Wing Chun techniques. If you look at most JKD guys you can see what was kept.

Don't you think that if all practitioners start applying the same principles, they may end up with a "style" or "system" very similar one to each other's? How does it fit here Bruce Lee's idea of "individuality" against the "uniformity" of a classical method or system?

"A principle is not a technique, and a lot of the techniques we focus on are also in many of the other arts. Some are probably working with them and not realizing it. Look at Jiu Jitsu - they train so much with alive sparring that they are using many of the same principles.

Just a few examples: They have simplified their techniques to be more efficient, they work on controlling the distance, they take what is offered them, and they work on understanding their opponent's structure and how to off balance it. But some may need to work on what may happen if they have to use their art in the street by working on staying on their feet.

The ground is a dangerous place in the street even against single opponent, who may be able to get to a knife when taken to the ground. Taking someone to the ground is not a great idea against multiple opponents.

It is a good idea for a grappler to spend time on standup striking and kicking as well as footwork."

How a martial artist using these principles can reach the level of individuality that makes him "more important than any system or method" like Bruce liked to say?

"If you really work to apply these principles with no thought as it is the "way" to do it in the art you study, you will be free from the cage that classical arts can put you in. After studying JKD for a while, I found that much of the martial arts that I learned in Taiwan was not as efficient or as practical as what I was learning in JKD, but some of it was very good and fit within the JKD structure. I kept what worked for me. When I teach

JKD I also show and teach what I found valuable in the other arts I have learned over the years. I just don't call it JKD or JKD concepts, I just call it by what it is. I also encourage our students to share what they have learned. We then analyze it for its strengths and weaknesses. It doesn't matter what style or system it is. We teach that there is no "way" but many "ways". Each student is free to find the best way that works.

What is the result you are after? Take knockout power in the straight lead. We had a student who didn't punch exactly right but had so much power that we didn't try and change it."

From a philosophical point of view, how the JKD philosophy can be applied to other arts?

"Understanding that as Krishnamurti taught, "The *Truth* is always out of all fixed patterns." Any style will by its very nature will have fixed patterns. The student of any art must learn to free himself from any boundary and be truly free to "express himself" and not just be a robot. I have found that the principles I have shared in this book can "liberate the student from the classical mess," as Bruce Lee said. I also realize that it is not that easy."

Finally, what it is that most important "idea" any martial artist can take from JKD and use in their chosen style?

JKD is a constant process of analysis. Analyze *what* to do, *how* to do it, *why* you are doing it, *when* and *when not* you should you do it, *what* is the best way to defend against it, and ask: *Is there a better way?*

Remember: Simplicity is the highest level of sophistication."

*"There is only one basic principle of self-defense:
You must apply the most effective weapon as soon
as possible to the most vulnerable target."*

– BRUCE LEE

NOTES

NOTES

www.ingramcontent.com/pod-product-compliance
Lightning Source LLC
Chambersburg PA
CBHW081743100526
44592CB00015B/2277